Learning English

GRUNDGRAMMATIK

NEUBEARBEITUNG

Übungsbuch

von
Rosemary Hellyer-Jones M. A.
und Peter Lampater

Ernst Klett Verlag
Stuttgart Düsseldorf Leipzig

Contents

Chapter 1 Nouns

1 All in the family ■ 1

Who is it? (Think carefully!)

"Young Willy's very much like his father, isn't he?"

1. Your uncle's son is your ________________.
2. Your aunt is your mother's or father's ________________.
3. Your mother's father is your ________________.
4. Your father's sisters are your ________________.
5. Your father is your grandparents' ________________,

   and your mother is your other grandparents' ________________.
6. Your sister's baby boy would be your ________________,

   and her baby girl would be your ________________.
7. Your father's brother is your ________________.
8. You are your grandmother's ________________.
9. If both your grandmothers have one son, one of them is your ________________

   and the other is your ________________.
10. The person you marry will be your ________________.
11. The man looking at this portrait says:

    "Brothers and sisters
    Have I none,
    But this man's father
    Is my father's son."

    The man is looking at a portrait of ________________.

2 Nouns and pronouns ■ 1, 2, 5

Which pronouns would you use with these nouns?
Whenever possible, give more than one answer.

he she it
we they

1. my father: *he*; 2. the family: ________; 3. your cousin: ________;

4. a friend: ________; 5. the fish: ________; 6. our team: ________;

7. a teacher: ________; 8. the secretary: ________; 9. a social worker: ________;

10. the waitress: ________; 11. the crowd: ________; 12. a child: ________;

13. our neighbour: ________; 14. the teenager: ________; 15. the sheep: ________;

16. a night nurse: ________; 17. the president: ________; 18. the deer: ________;

19. the Prime Minister: ________; 20. the lion: ________.

3 Using unusual nouns ■ 3

Complete the sentences with the correct nouns, verb forms and pronouns.

1. I can't find my  ______________. Have you seen __________ anywhere?
   – Yes, here __________ __________ *(be)*.

2. The  ______________ in that old house __________ *(be)* rather dangerous.
   – I know, __________ __________ *(be)* very steep and narrow.

3. What do you think of our new  ______________? Do you like __________?
   We bought __________ all at that new megastore on the Exeter Road.

4. I think we'd better call the  ______________. – I've already called __________.
   __________ __________ *(be)* on the way.

5. Did you know that the 

   ______________ __________ *(have)* a population of over 250 million?

6. We never watch the local  __________ on TV. – Don't you? We find __________ quite interesting sometimes.

7. What an awful subject 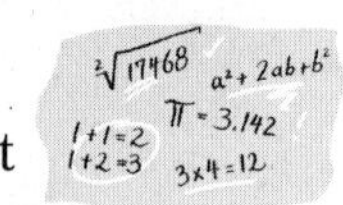

   ______________ __________ *(be)*. I hate __________!

8. Show me your new  ______________. – Here __________ __________ *(be)*. What do you think of __________? – __________ __________ *(look)* great. Where did you buy __________?

9. The  ______________ you lent me __________ *(not – cut)* very well, I'm afraid.

10. Your  __________ __________ *(look)* fantastic. Where did you have __________ done?

11.  __________ __________ *(taste)* best when __________ __________ *(be)* fresh from the garden.

12.  ______________ ______________ *(not – be used)* much for heating these days.

4 Different expressions for different things ■ 4

Use the right expression of quantity to describe these things.

1. two pairs of trousers

2. ______________________

3. ______________________

4. ______________________

5. ______________________

6. ______________________

7. ______________________

8. ______________________

9. ______________________

10. ______________________

⁂ 5 What's that in English? ■ 3, 4

Translate these sentences into English, being careful with the singular and plural forms and with the expressions of quantity.

1. Ich kann mich zwischen diesen zwei Hosen nicht entscheiden. Können Sie mir einen Rat geben?
2. Warum ist die Treppe zum ersten Stock gesperrt *(closed)*? Ich wollte zur Damenbekleidung. – Die Polizei ist da. Sie hat die Treppe gesperrt.
3. Brauchen wir sonst noch etwas? – Ein Brot, Milch, und vielleicht etwas Käse.
4. Ich war gerade beim Friseur. Gefallen dir meine Haare? – Tut mir leid, aber ich fand sie besser, als sie lang waren.
5. Wir müssen im Internet nachschauen. Die Informationen in diesem Fahrplan sind nicht detailliert genug.
6. Schau mal was ich gekauft habe! Zwei Jeans und eine tolle kurze Hose.

6 Regular and irregular plural forms ■ 5

Put the plural forms of these nouns in the correct rows.

aircraft ✔	*buffalo*	*church*	*foot*	*ox*	*thief*
baby ✔	*bus*	*country*	*hero ✔*	*photo*	*tomato*
beach ✔	*calf ✔*	*deer*	*knife*	*potato*	*tooth*
belief ✔	*cherry*	*dictionary*	*leaf*	*proof*	*video*
biro	*chief*	*enemy*	*life*	*roof*	*wolf*
box	*child ✔*	*fish*	*mouse*	*sheep*	*woman*

…s: beliefs, ______________________

…es / …oes: beaches, ______________ heroes, ______________

…ies: babies, ______________________

…ves: calves, ______________________

singular = plural: aircraft, ______________________

irregular forms: children, ______________________

⁂ 7 What is the difference? ■ 5

First try to do this without a dictionary. Then use an English-English dictionary to check.

1. What is the difference between the plural forms *fish* and *fishes*?
2. And between *fruit* and *fruits*?
3. What is the difference between *people* and *peoples*?
4. What is the difference between *crisis* and *crises*?
5. What are the plural forms of *passer-by* and *grown-up*?

Chapter 2 Personal and reflexive pronouns

1 Pronouns for persons ■ 7

Decide which personal pronoun to use in these sentences. (Some will be needed more than once.)

I me you he him she her it they them

1. Fred's very late. Maybe ________ 's not coming after all. – There's the doorbell. That's probably ________ now.
2. I don't like the look of that dog over there. ________ doesn't seem very friendly. – That's Sheila! ________ belongs to our neighbours. ________ needn't be afraid of ________.
3. Gary is a great basketball player. But his brother is better than ________ at football.
4. Everyone said how much ________ enjoyed our party last night.
5. If we see anyone along this road, we can ask ________ the way to the tennis courts.
6. Who are you playing against in the first round? – Anna. I won't have much chance against ________. She's a much better player than ________ am. And she's been playing much longer than ________, too.
7. Someone kept ringing me up last night, but when I answered the phone, ________ just hung up.

2 Trouble with the police ■ 7

Read the text and fill in the missing personal pronouns and possessive determiners. (There is often more than one correct solution.)

A motorist has been fined £20 for taking one hand off the steering wheel to eat a biscuit. Pat Storey, 33, says ________ was pulled up by police on the M3 for driving while not in proper control of ________ vehicle after ________ had seen ________ eating a chocolate biscuit. Pat had been taking ________ two children, James, 11, and Jacob, 2, to a birthday party when ________ was stopped near Winchester. ________ said that two officers told ________ that ________ had been driving at 68.7 mph in an area of roadworks limited to 50 mph but ________ equipment was not able to prove it. ________ said the police officers had told ________ that ________ had not stopped ________ for speeding but for driving while not in proper control of the vehicle. Pat said that ________ did a lot of driving in ________ job and that ________ hadn't taken the officers seriously. "I see everybody all the time talking on ________ mobile phones while ________ are steering and nobody stops ________."

(adapted from *The Times*)

3 Say it with "they" ■ 8

Rewrite the sentences without using the passive, to make them sound less formal.

1. The motorway has been closed.
   They've ...
2. A new bridge is being built over the Thames.
3. The new concert hall won't be finished before Christmas.
4. When is this road going to be widened?
5. Why weren't traffic lights put up here?
6. People are often caught for speeding on this stretch of road.
7. If less money had been spent on the new town hall, an open-air swimming pool could have been built.

"Let's enjoy it while we can – this is where they're going to build the new Leisure Centre."

4 *You* or *they*? ■ 8

Decide which general personal pronoun is needed.

1. __________ say it's unlucky to walk under a ladder. – Of course it is. Someone might drop something on __________, __________ never know!
2. Let me explain the rules of the game. First __________ throw the dice to see who's going to start ...
3. __________ have to be terribly careful at this roundabout. It's amazing that __________ haven't put traffic lights here.
4. How do __________ work this coffee machine?
5. I tried to get that CD, but I'm afraid __________'ve stopped producing it.
6. __________ ought not to believe everything __________ print in that stupid paper!

5 Do it yourself ■ 9

Finish what these people are saying, using self-*pronouns.*

1. Hey, you're riding your bike again. Did you find someone to repair it for you?
   – No, I didn't, so *I repaired it myself*.
2. I'm sorry. But I'm not going to do all that work for you two.
   You ____.
3. Your hair looks nice. Did you have it cut? – No, actually ______________________________.
4. Does your grandfather have anyone to look after him, do the cooking for him and so on?
   – Well, you wouldn't believe it, but ______________________________.
5. Can you help me tidy my room, Mum?
   – Sorry, I'm rather busy. You ______________________________.

6. Sheila is so shy; she just listens to what other people say and never ______________________.
7. Shall we ask Mrs Taylor to help us with this exercise?

   – I don't think that's necessary, ______________________.
8. There was only one person in the King's Rolls Royce.

   – Well, perhaps ______________________.

6 Yesterday ■ 9

Decide whether or not reflexive pronouns are needed.

1. I still ____________ very upset about yesterday. I ____________ with the bread knife, and Ken just ____________ as if nothing had ____________. – Did you ____________ badly? – Not really, but I still think Ken ____________ unfairly. And he still hasn't ____________.	*feel cut behave happen hurt act apologize*
2. What was Sandra's party like? Did you all ____________? – Yes, it was great. Her parents were there for the first twenty minutes or so. At first I ____________ if they were going to stay. But they didn't. They told us all to ____________ to food and drinks. Then they went out. So I needn't have ____________.	*enjoy wonder help worry*

⁂ 7 Rotkäppchen und Herr Wolf ■ 9

Translate the text into English. Remember that many reflexive verbs in German are not reflexive in English. Use a dictionary where necessary.

New York

Gestern abend war am Broadway die Premiere des Musicals *Little Red Riding Hood and the Wolf*. Bei der Story handelt es sich um eine sehr freie Version des bekannten Märchens:

Rotkäppchen ist auf dem Weg zu ihrer Großmutter, deren Haus **sich** in einem dunklen Wald **befindet**. Sie **beeilt sich**, da es bereits spät ist und sie **sich** im Dunkeln **fürchtet**. Plötzlich sieht sie, wie **sich** hinter den Bäumen etwas **bewegt**. Es ist ein junger Mann. Er **entschuldigt sich**, dass er sie erschreckt hat und sagt, sein Name sei Wolf. Rotkäppchen sieht seine großen traurigen grauen Augen und **verliebt sich** sofort in ihn. Sie **freut sich** darauf, ihn bald wieder zu sehen. Aber als sie **sich** am nächsten Abend an derselben Stelle im Wald wieder **treffen, hat sich** etwas Schreckliches **ereignet**. Der schöne Jüngling **hat sich** sehr **verändert**. Er sieht aus wie ein Wolf.

Rotkäppchen läuft zum Haus ihrer Großmutter. Diese liegt wie tot im Bett. Rotkäppchen kann **sich** nicht **vorstellen**, was passiert ist. Sie **fragt sich** verzweifelt, wie sie ihrer Großmutter helfen kann. Sie **fühlt sich** unsicher und kann **sich** nicht **entscheiden**, was sie tun soll. Plötzlich **öffnet sich** die Tür und der junge Mann tritt ein. Aber er kann **sich** nicht an sie **erinnern** und ... Nun, Sie werden **sich wundern!**

8 Mobile phones: Do you have one? ■ 10

Complete the sentences, using reflexive or reciprocal pronouns.

Summers/Orlando Sentinel

1. Today, more and more people send ____________________ e-mails or get to know ____________________ through the Internet. But even more people use mobile phones to communicate with ____________________.
2. You see – and hear – them everywhere. But people who use them in public sometimes make ____________________ unpopular. In the train, for example, travellers who are trying to make ____________________ comfortable on a long journey can find ____________________ irritated by the sound of other people's mobiles.
3. Of course, it is important and good for people to talk to ____________________. Mobiles can save lives, too. If you are alone in the woods, for example, fall and hurt ____________________ badly, a mobile is great to have in your pocket. But accidents have also been caused by drivers using their mobiles, injuring not only ____________________ but others on the road, too.

9 Different pronouns – different meanings ■ 6, 9, 10

Find the sentence parts that go together. (Notice the differences in meaning between the different pronouns.)

look after each other	*look after themselves*	*look after them*
talk to each other	*talk to themselves*	*talk to them*

1. When old friends meet, they love to ____________________.
2. People who are independent can ____________________.
3. They don't need anyone to ____________________.
4. People who live alone often start to ____________________.
5. First she was ill in bed, then he was, so they had to ____________________.
6. Budgies won't learn to talk if you don't ____________________.

Chapter 3 *S*-genitive, *of*-phrase and possessive words

1 By the seaside ■ 11, 12

Which is correct – s-genitive or of-phrase? (Put in **the** *where necessary.)*

1. Budleigh Salterton is a small seaside town in ______________________________ *(England / South West)*. 2. There are wonderful ______________________ *(coastline / views)* from ______________ ______________ *(cliffs / top)*. 3. Many of ____ *(residents / houses)* have sea views, too. 4. ________________________________ *(Mike / grandparents)* have a house in ________________________ *(town / middle)*. 5. Mike often stays at ________________ ___________________________ *(his grandparents / house)* in the summer holidays. 6. He enjoys taking ______________________________ *(his grandmother / two dogs)* for walks; they often have ______________________________ *(an hour / walk)* after breakfast, and if the weather is good, Mike spends ____________________ *(day / rest)* on the beach. 7. One of ____________________ ____________________ *(his grandfather / friends)* has a boat, and Mike sometimes goes fishing with him, right out into ______________________ *(bay / middle)*.

2 Where exactly? ■ 13

What kind of places or buildings are being referred to in these sentences?

office	*department store*	*shop*	*church*
restaurant	*café*	*cathedral*	*house*
surgery	*travel agency*		

1. I've got to go to the **doctor's** tomorrow. ______________
2. You can get your sunscreen at the **chemist's** over there. ______________
3. My sister is working at a **lawyer's** in George Street now. ______________
4. We looked round Westminster Abbey, but we didn't have time to go to **St Paul's**. ______________
5. Do you know where Sandy is? – She's at **Kim's**. ______________
6. Where's the wedding going to be? At **St Peter's**? ______________
7. **Watty's** is the best place to go if you want afternoon tea. ______________
8. Let's meet in the afternoon at **Harrod's**. ______________
9. The food at **Mario's** is fantastic! Have you been there yet? ______________
10. I collected the flight tickets at **Skinner's** this morning. ______________

3 Make up your mind, don't lose your head! ■ 14

Use these verbs and nouns to finish the sentences in a sensible way.

break change close fall off injure lose put ... in shake take off

arm bike eye head leg life mind pocket shoe

1. I'm afraid Tracey won't be able to play at the weekend. She ______ and finds it difficult to hold her racket.
2. Towards the end of the race Bob Sharkey, the American rider, had a bad crash. He ______ ______ and ______.
3. Every year there are serious accidents in the mountains. Many people ______ because they take unnecessary risks.
4. Before we entered the mosque, we ______.
5. We always thought the weather in England was awful. But after that fantastic holiday in Cornwall, we ______.
6. He asked her whether she wanted to come to the party, but she ______.
7. I simply wanted to concentrate on the music, so I leaned back in my chair and ______ ______.
8. If your hands are cold and you haven't got any gloves, you'd better ______ ______.

⁂ 4 Mein Opa ■ 14

✎ *Translate this text into English. These expressions will help you:*

lose one's balance owe one's life to s.o. make up one's mind
love s.o. with all one's heart get on s.o.'s nerves bare one's teeth

Mein Großvater ist 78 und unmöglich. Letztes Jahr fiel er vom Motorrad und brach sich den Arm. Im Herbst kletterte er auf eine Leiter, um Äpfel zu pflücken. Ein starker Wind blies ihm ins Gesicht, und plötzlich verlor er das Gleichgewicht. Er fiel herunter und brach sich das Bein. Letzte Woche wollte er seine Autositze mit Benzin reinigen. Dabei steckte er die Pfeife an. Meine Großmutter rettete ihn aus der brennenden Garage. Er verdankt ihr das Leben.

Gestern stand er da, die Hände in den Taschen, die Pfeife (eine neue) im Mund, und sagte: „Ich habe mich entschlossen, den Mount Everest zu besteigen." (Er scheint nicht zu wissen, wie viele Menschen dort schon ums Leben gekommen sind.)
Meine Großmutter muss ihn von ganzem Herzen lieben. Ihr scheint er nicht auf die Nerven zu gehen. Nur der Hund der Nachbarn fletscht die Zähne, wenn er meinen Großvater sieht.

5 My own TV ■ 15

Say what these people have or would like to have.
Use possessive determiners + **own**.

1. Mark's parents hope he will become a great tennis player. When he was only five he had his own tennis court / a tennis court of his own.

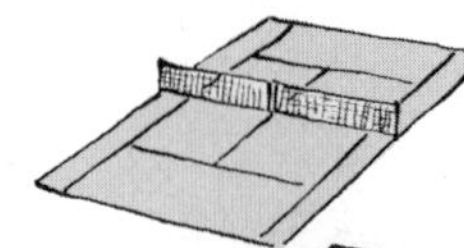

2. In the summer, I can go over to the neighbours' for a swim. You know, they ____________________.

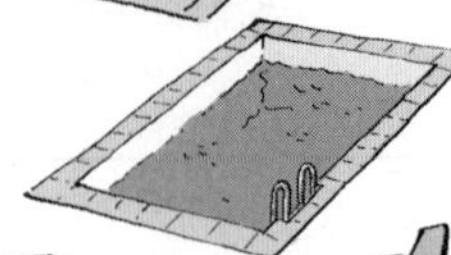

3. Mike Dillon, the Hollywood star, won't have to wait at airports any more. He ____________________.

4. Lots of families argue about which programme to watch. The problem would be solved if everyone ____________________.

5. Sheila enjoys riding very much. But her parents aren't wealthy enough to buy her ____________________.

6. After working for the company for over twenty years, John has finally left. Now he ____________________.

7. Even before they get their driving licence, most teenagers dream of having ____________________.

6 Yours or mine? ■ 14, 16

Fill in the correct possessive determiners and possessive pronouns.

1. I've forgotten ________ pocket calculator. Could I use ________, Emma? – Sorry, but ________ doesn't work any more. Ask Robert. Look, he's got ________.
2. Where are Jane and Fiona? ________ schoolbags are over there in the corner. – I don't think those are ________, ________ are far older.
3. Do these bikes belong to you two? – No, those aren't ________ bikes, ________ are in the bicycle shed.
4. Have you got ________ maths homework, Jenny? I couldn't do ________. Can I have a look at ________? – I don't think ________ is correct either. You'd better ask Kate, ________ is usually perfect.
5. Can you give me back that book of ________ some time, John? – I've got a book of ________? Oh yes, I remember now. I'll bring it to school tomorrow.

Chapter 4 Articles and demonstratives

1 Be careful with *the* ■ 17–19

Fill in the definite article where necessary.

1. Do you like ______ Italian food? If so, you'll love ______ food at that new Italian restaurant.
2. I've just started a book about ______ life of Henry VIII. It gives a very interesting picture of ______ 16th century life.
3. I usually take ______ bus to ______ school in ______ winter months, but I often go by ______ bike when it gets warmer.
4. Did you have ______ lunch on ______ plane? – Yes, but it wasn't as good as ______ lunch we had when we went to ______ Netherlands by ______ plane ______ last spring.
5. Can you tell me ______ way to ______ Buckingham Palace from here? – Go down ______ Queen Victoria Street until you get to ______ underground station. You can get to Westminster by ______ underground, and then walk to ______ palace through ______ St James's Park.
6. ______ Burtons can't come to ______ supper on ______ Friday after all – ______ poor Mrs Burton is ill.

2 Describing people ■ 20, 44

Use nouns to describe what jobs these people (would like to) have, where they come from or what they believe in.

1. My brother has always been interested in machines. He works at a garage. – *He's a mechanic.*
2. My sister is working in a boutique at the moment, selling clothes. – She …
3. My cousin loves the theatre. After school he wants to go to drama school. – He …
4. Arazi comes from Iran. His religion is Islam, and his God is called Allah. – He …
5. One of the English teachers at our school is from Edinburgh. – She …
6. Patrick's mother designed the new cafeteria. – She …
7. My grandpa has been a member of the Labour Party for ages. He still believes that private capital is evil and that the government should own industries. – He …
8. He always has long arguments with my grandmother, who thinks that wealth and property should be owned privately. – She …
9. My father's best friend lives in Cardiff. – His best friend …

3 How much? How fast? How often? ■ 21

Look at the pictures and say how much these things cost, how often things are done, etc.

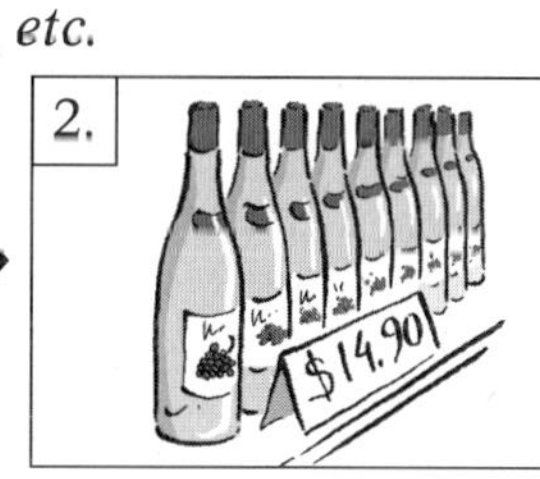

1. *The strawberries are / cost $1.50 a pound.*
2. ______________________________ →
____

3. ______________________________
____
4. ______________________________ →
____

5. ______________________________________

____

6. ______________________________________

____

→

⁂ 4 In London ■ 17–21

Put in **the** *or* **a / an** *where it is needed.*

a) ______ sight of ______ Houses of Parliament viewed from ______ bus crossing ______ River Thames at ______ Westminster Bridge makes ______ most British people feel patriotic and proud. Some people have ______ pleasure of seeing it five times ______ week, on their way to ______ work. But ______ people tend to forget that ______ Palace of Westminster is in ______ fact ______ place of work for over 1,700 people. Rather like ______ small village, ______ palace contains not only ______ chambers of ______ House of Commons and ______ House of Lords, as well as ______ offices of MPs and Lords, but also ______ bars, ______ restaurants, ______ gymnasium, ______ hair salon and ______ travel agency.

b) But ______ Tower of London is undoubtedly ______ capital's greatest historical sight. Today ______ Tower is famous as ______ tourist attraction, but at ______ different times in ______ past, it has been used as ______ fortress, ______ royal palace, ______ prison and ______ place of execution. Many of ______ people who came to ______ Tower as ______ prisoners were brought there by ______ boat. Two of ______ most famous prisoners were Anne Boleyn and Catherine Howard, ______ both of whom were wives of ______ King Henry VIII. Although they were ______ queens, they were sentenced to ______ death and lost their heads here. In ______ 16th century, ______ life was hard for ______ most people; even ______ life of ______ queen was not always safe for long!

c) In London, ______ public transport is excellent. Going by ______ underground is ______ fastest way to travel around. But if you take ______ bus, you can see some of ______ sights on ______ way. On ______ other hand, there is usually ______ heavy traffic on ______ streets of London. If you want to go from ______ Marble Arch to ______ British Museum, for ______ example, you'll be quicker on ______ underground than on ______ bus taking you along ______ Oxford Street!

5 Saying it differently ■ 22

Make sentences with the definite or the indefinite article, so the meaning stays the same.

both such twice half too what quite all

1. The programme goes on for thirty minutes. → *The programme goes on for half an hour.*
2. Well, this is a surprise! → Well, …
3. Of the hundred dollars he had, he spent fifty.→ He spent …
4. I've got about 40 CDs, but Tim's got at least 80. → Tim …
5. Nobody wanted to go home. The party was so good! → It was …
6. What do you think of my idea? Is it good? – It's not a bad idea. → It's …
7. Shall we play this piece – and that piece, too? – Yes, let's. → Let's play …
8. There's no more cream. Has Susan given it all to the cat? → Has …
9. Don't put the butter in a place that's too warm. → Don't …
10. If I buy a bar of chocolate, I usually only eat half. → I usually …

6 Was für eine Aussicht! ■ 22

Translate the text into English.

Es war ein schöner Morgen, als ich am Empire State Building ankam. Die Schlange vor den Kartenschaltern schien schon eine halbe Meile lang zu sein. Aber später am Tag sind dort doppelt so viele Besucher. Die Aussichtsplattform *(observatory)* befindet sich fast eine viertel Meile oberhalb der Fifth Avenue. Was für eine fantastische Aussicht! Wie schade, dass es inzwischen wolkig geworden war. An wolkenfreien Tagen kann man doppelt so weit sehen. Jemand sagte, dass es in New York die halbe Zeit neblig sei.
Alle Touristen waren begeistert *(full of enthusiasm)* und machten viele Fotos. Doch die ganze Zeit klingelten Handys *(mobile phones)*. Ich blieb eine halbe Stunde dort oben. Als ich mit dem Aufzug wieder hinunterfuhr, traf ich Fritz aus Neustadt. Was für eine Überraschung.

7 That was stupid, wasn't it? ■ 23

Fill in **this**, **that**, **these** *or* **those**.

"What about all those times we left before the meter ran out?"

You know where we parked the car ________ morning? I can't remember the name of ________ street. Do you remember it?

– Sorry, no. ________ street names here all sound the same, don't they? But didn't we leave it somewhere behind ________ park over there?

– Wait, let's look at ________ big street plan here. Now, ________ is the way we've come. And is ________ 22nd Street back there?

– Yes, it says S 22nd.

– Hm, well, let's ask someone. Look at ________ patrol car parked across the street. ________ officers are sure to help us find the car. I read somewhere that police officers ________ days are specially trained to deal with people like us.

– By the way, do you still have the car keys? – Of course, let me just check. Oh no, where are they?

Chapter 5 Expressions of quantity

1 Lost at sea in a dinghy[1] ■ 24, 25

some any something anything someone anyone somewhere anywhere

Put in the right word.

Imagine being in a rubber dinghy ____________ in the middle of the Atlantic Ocean for six days, without food or water. It may sound like ____________ from an adventure story. But it really happened to Jenny Clark and her boyfriend Tim Davidson. The two young people had never experienced ____________ so terrible.

The horror trip began ____________ hours after they had started on a sailing holiday. They were out in a yacht ____________ miles off the coast of Spain when ____________ exploded in the engine room. Then the boat caught fire. "It happened so quickly," says Jenny. "There wasn't ____________ ____________ could do."

Soon they were both in the rubber dinghy. "We didn't have ____________ time to put ____________ food in the dinghy," explains Tim. "There wasn't even ____________ chance to send an SOS." The yacht quickly went up in flames and sank.

The six days in the dinghy were a nightmare. They didn't have ____________ to eat and they didn't have ____________ drinking water. "But we were lucky," says Jenny. "On ____________ of the days it rained, so at least we could catch ____________ of the rainwater."

Soon the weather got worse. "____________ once told me you get ____________ pretty big waves in the Atlantic," says Tim. "I think ____________ of the waves out there were 30 feet high or more. I've never seen ____________ like it ____________."

Five ships passed before they were saved. "We waved and shouted, hoping desperately for ____________ to notice us," says Jenny. "But we couldn't get ____________'s attention. In the end ____________ saw us. It was the sixth ship – and our sixth day in the dinghy."

[1] **dinghy** ['dɪŋgɪ] *Schlauchboot*

"They're going on: the idiots must think we're on some damn-fool Atlantic crossing stunt."

2 Questions with a difference ■ 24, 25

Decide whether to use **some** *(compounds with* **some***) or* **any** *(compounds with* **any***) in these questions.*

1. Could I have ______________ more coffee, please?
2. These biscuits are home-made. Would you like ______________?
3. Have you got ______________ orange juice to drink? If so, could you give me ______________?
4. Can I offer you ______________ to drink?
5. Two pounds of apples. ______________ else?
6. Are you going ______________ interesting in the holidays?
7. Shall we have a holiday ______________ in Italy next spring?
8. Do you know ______________ about that accident yesterday? Was ______________ hurt?
9. Let's go to the cinema. Are there ______________ good films on this week?
10. Could ______________ please clean the floor? – I'll do it. But could you give me ______________ to clean it with?

3 What's that in English? ■ 26

a) *Translate these sentences into English, using* **no**, **none**, **nothing, nobody** *or* **nowhere**.

1. Leider habe ich keine Zeit, mein Zimmer jetzt aufzuräumen.
2. Sind keine Briefmarken mehr im Haus? In dieser Schublade sind keine.
3. Ich machte die Tür auf, aber es war keiner da.
4. Wir können die Party bei mir zu Hause machen. Meine Eltern haben nichts dagegen.
5. Ich kann meine Schlüssel nicht finden. Sie sind nirgends hier.

b) *Now rewrite the sentences, using* **not** … **any**, **not** … **anything**, *etc. to replace these constructions. The meaning should remain the same.*

4 Sceptical questions ■ 27

Ask questions with **how much** *or* **how many.**

1. When I was in America in the holidays, I visited most of the National Parks.
   Well, how many National Parks did you visit?
2. I climbed some very high mountains in Yellowstone National Park.
3. And I saw quite a few grizzly bears.
4. I walked down the Grand Canyon and up again. It only took me a few hours.
5. But it was very hot, so I drank masses of water.
6. I must have driven thousands of miles on that trip.
7. I had this big American car, automatic, of course. It used quite a bit of gas.
8. In Las Vegas I went to all the casinos.
9. And I won masses of money.
10. I took lots of photographs.

5 Little time and few chances ■28

Make these sentences sound more colloquial by replacing **(a) little, few, fewer** *and* **less** *by equivalent expressions, e.g.* **(not) much, (not) many, some, not enough.**

1. In the match on Saturday, United had **few chances** to score.
   In the match on Saturday, United didn't have many chances to score.
2. There was **little** work to be done, so we went home after only an hour.
3. She is often on her own. She seems to have **few** friends.
4. There are **few** people nowadays who don't know how to work with a computer.
5. She is very busy all week and spends **little** time with her children.
6. I have **less** time today than I had yesterday.
7. Today **fewer** people smoke cigarettes than 20 years ago.
8. This Christmas I spent **less** than last year. I simply bought **fewer** presents, so I've got **a little** money left.
9. If you have **a little** time, look at some of the museums in Washington. – I'm afraid I'll have **too little** time for sightseeing.
10. There was **little** interest in the film, and very **few** people came to see it.

⁂ 6 A little is better than hardly any ■24, 26, 27, 28

Rewrite these sentences using the following expressions. (There is usually more than one possibility.)

any
a bit of
hardly any
a few
a little
very few
very little
a lot of
lots of
(not) many
(not) much
no
plenty of

1. We only did three word tests last term.
   We did very few / We did hardly any / We didn't do many word tests last term.
2. He spends more than £1,000 on clothes every year.
3. There's enough time. The concert begins at 8.30, and it's 7 o'clock now.
4. A small glass of wine every day is very good for you.
5. All the milk's gone, and nearly all the yoghurt.
6. There are still six pieces of cake left.
7. Liza has about 200 CDs, but only about five are worth listening to.
8. There is half a pound of butter in the fridge and three eggs.
9. I went shopping this morning. Now I've got about a pound left.

7 Games ■29

Decide whether to use **every** *(compounds with* **every***) or* **any** *(compounds with* **any***) in these sentences.*

1. ______________ child enjoys playing games, and so do most adults.
2. In most card games, ______________ starts with the same number of cards in their hand.
3. In some games, such as chess, the rules are the same ______________, while in others they vary from place to place.
4. Bridge can only be played by four players. But in a lot of games, such as Monopoly, ______________ number of players between two and six or more can take part.
5. In games of skill like chess, the best player will normally win, but in games where chance plays a big part, ______________ may win!
6. Lots of people enjoy quiz games, where questions may be asked about practically ______________.

7. It's best to avoid games that are played for large sums of money. There are people who have lost ______________ they had!
8. There are lots of games, like guessing games, that need no equipment at all, which is good because you can play them ______________ you happen to be.

8 Museum etiquette ■ 24, 26, 28, 29, 30

Fill in these expressions of quantity.

all✓ all all all all all the any any any any everybody a few few no no none

We *all* want you to enjoy your visit here at the Buffalo Bill Historical Center. For the sake of our present and future visitors, however, we have rules that ______________ must observe. We hope that these ______________ rules do not cause ______________ inconvenience.

- ◆ For the comfort of ______________ visitors, and the protection of our collection, the Historical Center is a non-smoking facility.
- ◆ As almost ______________ human body oils are acidic[1], ______________ of the works of art should be touched. But there are ______________ objects in the Historical Center that are touchable and identified as such. ______________ others should not be handled in ______________ way.
- ◆ Strollers[2] are provided for our small visitors, but they should be under the control of an adult ______________ time.
- ◆ ______________ pets are allowed in the museum, so please leave them outside.
- ◆ Do not bring ______________ weapons into the Historical Center.
- ◆ Leave ______________ backpacks, motorcycle helmets, umbrellas and large containers in your car or check them into free lockers near the front door.
- ◆ ______________ museum visitors are required to wear shirts and shoes; ______________ bathing suits in the museum, please.

(adapted from a leaflet from the Buffalo Bill Historical Center)

[1] **acidic** *sauer* – [2] **stroller** *Kinderwagen*

9 Parallel Lives ■ 31

Fill in the right word. **both the two two neither either**

The Daily Globe offers all its readers the chance to contact long-lost relatives and friends. Each week we will present the story of someone reunited with their loved one. This incredible tale is about THE PARALLEL LIVES of ________ people reunited through this newspaper.

We've had many happy endings before but none of them quite matches this one.

In the fifties ________ young people, Steve Smith and Gillian Potter, were still at school. ________ went to Hargrove School in Bristol, and started going out together when they were 15 and 16. ________ years later they got engaged[1]. But then Steve went abroad and ________ gradually drifted apart. ________ was very keen on writing, so in the end they lost contact and the engagement was broken off.

There have been extraordinary parallels in their lives. ________ had happy but short marriages, which ________ came to an end when their partners were killed in traffic accidents in the very same year. Gillian and Steve ________ have one son. ________ young men are keen on rugby and they ________ play for their county.

Gillian and Steve have been living on their own for exactly fifteen years now. ________ has ever thought of getting married again. They ________ used to work in the banking business and retired last year.

Our paper traced Gillian, who lives in North London, through her sister. Then Steve, who later returned to Bristol, went to visit his old sweetheart – after 44 years.

When we talked to Gillian she said, "We were ________ rather lonely people. Now there is a lovely second chance for ________ of us." She doesn't know yet whether they will live together in Bristol or in London. "________ place will be fine." she smiled.

[1] **to get engaged** *sich verloben*

⁂ 10 Stay at the Belmont ■ 27–31

Translate this hotel brochure into English, paying particular attention to the expressions of quantity.

- Das Belmont in Chicago ist das ideale Hotel für **alle** Reisenden und Geschäftsleute.
- Es gibt **viel** zu sehen in Chicago, und **viele** der berühmtesten Sehenswürdigkeiten sind zu Fuß oder mit dem Taxi zu erreichen. Außerdem gibt es für unsere Gäste einen Pendelbus *(shuttle bus)* zur Stadtmitte: Abfahrt **alle** 20 Minuten vom Haupteingang (Michigan Avenue).
- Die LaSalle Street, das finanzielle Zentrum der Stadt, ist nur **ein paar** Häuserblocks entfernt, und zum Ufer *(shore)* des Michigan Sees sind es nur **ein paar** Minuten durch den Grant Park.
- Aber eigentlich braucht **niemand** das Hotel zu verlassen. Die fünf Geschäfte im Erdgeschoss verkaufen Geschenkartikel *(gifts)* und Luxusartikel *(luxury goods)* **jeder** Art.
- Die **beiden** Restaurants im 10. Stock sind für ihre ausgezeichnete Küche *(food)* berühmt. **Beide** werden von bekannten französischen Köchen *(chefs)* geleitet.
- **Alle** unsere Zimmer haben einen fantastischen Blick auf den See, und **jedes einzelne** ist luxuriös eingerichtet *(furnished)*. **Viele** haben sogar zwei separate Badezimmer.

⇨ Unsere **beiden** riesigen Konferenzsäle *(conference rooms)* stehen Ihnen ebenso zur Verfügung *(to be at s.o.'s disposal)* wie die **vielen** kleineren Räume. So sind wir in der Lage, **jedes** Ereignis zu organisieren, von kleinen geschäftlichen Zusammenkünften bis zu gigantischen Ausstellungen *(exhibitions)*.

11 A puzzle ■ 24–31

a) Do the puzzle by completing the proverbs and other expressions.

Across:
4. There is an exception to ... rule.
6. There is ... new under the sun.
7. Many are called, but ... are chosen.
10. ... cats are grey in the dark.
11. You can't have the best of ... worlds.
12. Too ... cooks spoil the broth.
13. "I've been looking ... for you!"
15. You never get ... for nothing.
17. "Not me and not you" = "... of us"
19. You can't please ...
20. "Is there a bottle opener ...?"

Down:
1. "A thousand dollars is a ... of money."
2. "Don't rush, we've got ... of time."
3. ... excuse is better than none.
5. "Which of the two do you want?" – "I don't want ..."
6. "Where is the damn thing? It's ... here!"
8. There are ... so blind as those who will not see.
9. "It's not mine. It belongs to ... else."
10. If ... can go wrong, it will.
12. You can have too ... of a good thing.
14. A ... of what you fancy does you good.
16. There's ... smoke without fire.
18. "Every one of us" – "... of us"

✎ *b) Now put the proverbs into German. (Use an equivalent proverb in German if you know one.)*

Chapter 6 Prepositions in expressions of time and place

1 Special days ■ 36.1 + 2

Choose the correct prepositions.

in at on

1. Small children are always very excited ___ Christmas time. In Britain, they don't get their presents ___ Christmas Eve, but ___ Christmas Day. When they go to bed ___ the evening of Christmas Eve, a lot of children try to stay awake. They know that Santa Claus always comes down the chimney late ___ night with their presents, but when? Will he come ___ midnight this year? Or ___ one o'clock ___ the morning?
   Then, ___ the morning of December 25th, when they wake up and find their presents at the foot of the bed, they realize they must have fallen asleep ___ the night, *before* he came, just like the year before!
2. Easter is ___ March this year. ___ Good Friday we sometimes go to church. There is a special service that starts ___ noon and finishes ___ 3 o'clock ___ the afternoon.
3. My birthday is ___ July. It's nice to have it ___ the summer, because I usually have a party ___ my birthday, and we sometimes have a barbecue. It stays light nice and long ___ the evenings ___ that time of the year.

2 What's that in English? ■ 36

Translate these sentences.

1. Mein Zug fährt am Montag um halb zehn.
2. Ich werde nur drei Tage [lang] weg sein.
3. Beeil dich, bitte. Wir wollten doch bis spätestens viertel vor acht gehen.
4. Ich war seit Wochen nicht mehr im Kino.
5. Wie lange wohnt ihr schon hier? – Seit September. Wir sind vor genau acht Wochen umgezogen.
6. Möchten Sie den Termin am Vormittag, oder kommen Sie lieber nachmittags zwischen drei und vier?
7. Im nächsten Winter möchte ich wieder zum Skifahren.
8. Bleiben Sie bis Neujahr? – Ja, wir bleiben vom Donnerstag bis zum Dienstag. Wir reisen erst am 2. Januar ab.

3 On the train ■ 37

Use prepositions of place and direction to complete the text. (Sometimes there is more than one correct solution.)

Jack had got ______ the train ______ Reading. At first he had been on his own, but ______ the next stop some people had come ______ his compartment, an elderly couple. They had put their luggage ______ the rack ______ Jack's head: two large suitcases and a birdcage, balanced ______ the smaller of the cases.

It looked dangerous. If the train braked suddenly, it might fall down and crash _______ Jack's head. The man was sitting _______ the window, his wife _______ him. They had a large, angry-looking dog with them. It was lying _______ the floor _______ the man's legs, its open mouth uncomfortably _______ Jack's ankles. There was a No Smoking sign _______ the opposite wall. The man took a large cigar _______ a leather case, lit it and blew the smoke straight _______ Jack's face. Jack got up, almost fell _______ the dog, and then stepped _______ its tail. He just managed to get _______ the compartment, the dog furiously barking _______ the door.

The train was going _______ a hill now, moving slowly _______ its tracks. It was peaceful _______ the next compartment. Jack looked _______ the window. It was a wonderful morning, not a single cloud _______ the sky. The train was going _______ a small farm. He noticed some cows _______ a field and an old tractor parked _______ a fence. Some large black birds were sitting _______ the fence. A farmer was walking _______ the field _______ the cows. A small dog ran _______ him, sometimes looking back at its slow master. Jack closed his eyes and started to dream.

The farmer's little dog jumped _______ the fence and started to run _______ the train. And it was getting bigger and bigger. It caught up with the train and ran _______ Jack's carriage now. And then it jumped and crashed _______ the window, pushed Jack _______ the wall, its great white teeth _______ his throat.

He screamed. There was a strange man _______ him. "Tickets please," said the ticket collector. "Everything OK, sir?"

4 *By* or *with*? *After* or *behind*? ■ 36, 37

Translate the sentences, using these prepositions:

after among at behind between by (up) to (not) until with

1. Der Polizist lief hinter dem Einbrecher her, verlor ihn aber aus den Augen *(to lose sight of s.o.)*, weil sich der Einbrecher hinter einem Baum versteckt hatte.
2. Robin Hood verteilte *(to share out)* das gestohlene Geld immer unter den Armen.
3. Zu der Zeit gab es große soziale Unterschiede zwischen den normannischen Herrschern und den Angelsachsen.
4. Eric wohnte viele Jahre lang bei seinen Großeltern in Australien. Und die Sommerferien verbrachte er oft bei seiner Tante in Sydney.
5. Die Eltern sagten, ich sollte auf das Baby bis 10 Uhr aufpassen, aber sie kamen erst um 12 Uhr nach Hause.
6. Ich bleibe nicht lange in der Stadt. Ich bin bis (spätestens) halb vier wieder hier.

Chapter 7 Adjectives

1 Asleep or sleeping? ■ 38

Choose from these adjectives to complete the sentences.

living alive alone lone afraid frightened asleep sleeping

1. ______________ children can sometimes be very difficult to wake.
2. The bank robber told the ______________ customers to stand against the wall.
3. It was half past two in the morning. Everybody in the house was ______________.
4. When John got off the train, he saw a ______________ figure standing at the other end of the platform.
5. Certain types of fish are often sold while they are still ______________.
6. After the accident, he was ______________ of driving on the motorway again for a while.
7. "The ______________ Desert" was one of Walt Disney's most successful nature films.
8. Some people enjoy being ______________, and never feel lonely.

2 It didn't taste too bad! ■ 39

Complete the text, choosing from the verbs and the adjectives on the right. (There may be more than one correct solution.)

be feel get go grow look sound seem smell taste

alright dark delicious exciting funny green hungry quiet sick oily strong upset

The idea of going to this old fish and chip shop didn't ______________ very ______________. But Marion had asked me to come and she always ______________ when people don't want to do what she suggests. So I went, although I didn't ______________ at all.

It was fairly late, and it was already ______________ when we got near the shop. We could soon tell we were getting near the shop because it ______________ so ______________. But the food ______________, and the fish actually ______________. (The chips ______________ a little ______________, though.) When I had eaten about half of it, I started to ______________. Marion said, "Your face has ______________, I hope you won't ______________."

"Oh, ______________, Marion," I said and ran to the door.

3 Everything all right? ■ 39

✎ *Translate the text into English, deciding whether to use adjectives or adverbs for the marked words.*

Alles schien so **schön** und **harmonisch**, als Sarah plötzlich sagte: „Diese Suppe riecht **komisch**, oder?“ „Ich weiß nicht. Mit meiner Erkältung kann ich nicht sehr **gut** riechen. Schmeckt sie auch **komisch**?“ Sie nahm ihren Löffel und probierte die Suppe **langsam** und **gründlich**. „Sie schmeckt **abscheulich**. Rufen wir die Kellnerin.“ Die Kellnerin war sehr **langsam**, und ich sah, wie Sarah **wütend** wurde. „Bleib **ruhig**,“ sagte ich. Die Kellnerin kam an unseren Tisch. Sie sah **ernst** aus und schaute uns **kritisch** an, schien sich aber **unsicher** zu fühlen. „Ist alles in Ordnung?“ fragte sie. Ihre Stimme klang nicht sehr **freundlich**.

4 The comparison of adjectives ■ 40

Basic form	*Comparative form*	*Superlative form*
cheap *expensive*	*cheaper* *more expensive*	*cheapest* *most expensive*

"Or, if you want something more expensive, I can show you this again tomorrow."

✏ *Make a table like the one above and write down the three forms of these adjectives:*

astonishing bad big busy clever far fit good late many much narrow quiet simple

5 The greatest sporting show on Earth ■ 40, 41

Since they began in 1896, the modern Olympic Games have been about superlatives – the best, the fastest, the greatest. And every city that hosts the Games tries to make the show bigger, better and more spectacular than ever before. The most dramatic event every time is the Men's 100 meter race, although it lasts for less than ten seconds!

✏ *a) Say what you think of these Olympic events. Compare four of the pairs shown in the pictures. You can choose from these adjectives and phrases.*

good exciting tough spectacular dramatic interesting to watch easy to follow

Example: *1. I think athletics is more interesting to watch than cycling. / I don't think cycling is as interesting to watch as athletics. / I find athletics just as interesting as cycling.*

✏ *b) Which Olympic events do you like best? Write a few sentences explaining why you think they are the most exciting / the most dramatic / ...*

c) *Look at the cartoon carefully. Then answer these questions, using comparative and superlative forms.*

1. hat is the difference between a normal bicycle race and a slow-bicycle race?
2. Why is everybody waiting? What has happened to the winner of the gold medal?

"I still feel that the Olympics is no place for slow-bicycle racing."

6 What's that in English? ■ 39–41, 43

Translate these sentences into English.

1. Je heißer der Tag wird, desto anstrengender wird der Marathonlauf.
2. In den letzten Jahren wurden die Spiele immer spektakulärer und die Teilnehmerzahl *(number of competitors)* immer größer.
3. Obwohl der 100-Meter-Lauf kürzer als alle anderen Läufe ist, sind die Vorbereitungen und das Training genauso wichtig wie bei den längeren Strecken *(distances)*.
4. Von allen olympischen Disziplinen *(events)* finden viele das Synchronschwimmen *(synchronized swimming)* am wenigsten interessant.
5. Das Wichtigste bei den Olympischen Spielen ist nicht zu gewinnen, sondern teilzunehmen. *(Pierre de Coubertin)*

7 Yellowstone National Park ■ 40, 41

Use the superlative forms of the given adjectives to complete the text. Decide whether to use **the** *or not. (Sometimes there is more than one correct solution.)*

dangerous exciting famous forceful frequent great high impressive large old popular spectacular

✿ Yellowstone has been a national park since 1872. In fact it is ____________________ in the USA.

✿ It has ____________________ concentration of wildlife in the lower mainland USA (with buffalo and grizzly bears being ____________________ but also ____________________ among them).

✿ While Yellowstone has become ____________________ of America's national parks, its popularity has at the same time become ____________________ threat to its environment.

✿ Yellowstone's ____________________ mountain is Mount Washburn (10,243 feet), and the Grand Canyon of the Yellowstone is one of ____________________ canyons in the world.

✿ Yellowstone has the world's ____________________ active geyser field, and its ____________________ geyser is Old Faithful.

✿ One of the Yellowstone geysers is called Steamboat. Steamboat's eruptions are ____________________ in the world, with steam and water shooting up to over 300 feet.

✿ But while Old Faithful's eruptions are ____________________ (an eruption occurs about every 80 minutes), Steamboat erupts very irregularly – only twice in the last ten years.

8 This one and that one ■ 42

Complete the sentences logically, using the prop word **one** / **ones** *together with suitable adjectives.*

1. Emma is 15. Her two sisters are 17 and 12. She has two sisters, an older one and a younger one.
2. Tibby is black and Toby is grey. We have two cats, ____________________
3. This pullover cost £50, and that pullover cost only £20. I bought two pullovers, ____________________
4. St Peter's Church was built in the 13th century, St Mary's in about 1400, and St Mark's in 1995.
   There are three churches in town, two ____________________
5. These trousers are size 12, and those trousers over there are size 10.
   These don't feel as tight as ____________________
6. The walk across the moors is ten miles, and the cliff walk is six.
   Which walk shall we take, ____________________

9 Famous sayings ■ 43

Complete the sentences, choosing from these expressions.

the blind
the blind
the blind
the hungry
the old
the poor
the rich
the rich
the young

a blind wife
a deaf husband
a rich man
a rich man
the rich man
the poor man
the one-eyed man

1. If you can actually count your money, then you are not really ____________________. *(J. Paul Getty)*
2. There is one law for ____________________, and one law for ____________________. *(Proverb)*
3. He has filled ____________________ with good things, and ____________________ he has sent empty away. *(The Bible)*
4. ____________________ has his ice in the summer, and ____________________ gets his in the winter. *(Proverb)*
5. It is easier for a camel to go through the eye of a needle than for ____________________ to enter the kingdom of heaven. *(The Bible)*
6. When ____________________ lead ____________________, both shall fall into the ditch. *(Proverb)*
7. In the country of ____________________, ____________________ is king. *(Proverb)*
8. ____________________ and ____________________ are always a happy couple. *(Proverb)*
9. It's all that ____________________ can do for ____________________, to shock them and keep them up to date. *(G. B. Shaw)*

✎ *b) Translate sentences 4, 5, 7 and 8 into German.*

10 Quick translation ■ 43

Say what these are in English.

1. Jugendliche
2. der Kleine
3. die Tote
4. ein Blinder
5. viele Behinderte
6. zwei Schwarze
7. die Arbeitslosen
8. die Lebenden und die Toten
9. eine Gruppe von Obdachlosen
10. das Schlimme daran
11. die Konservativen
12. ein Kranker

11 Countries, people and languages ■ 44

Complete this list of countries, their inhabitants and languages.

Country	Individual person	The people in general speak these languages
1. Australia	an Australian	The Australians speak English.
2. Belgium		
3. Britain		
4.	a Canadian	
5. China		
6.	a Dane	
7. England		
8. France		
9.	a German	
10. Ireland		
11.	an Italian	
12. the Netherlands		
13.	a Pole	
14. Portugal		
15.	a Turk	
16. the USA		
17.	a Welshman / a Welshwoman	

1 Adjective or adverb? ■ 45, 46

a) Fill in the correct form.

How music can drive motorists ____________ *(crazy)*

Road rage is an ____________ *(enormous)* problem in Britain. It is ____________ *(good)* known that our drivers are among the most ____________ *(aggressive)* in Europe. Many like to drive ____________ *(fast)*, and at the same time they like to listen to ____________ *(deafening)* ____________ *(loud)* music. Experts warn that this is ____________ *(actual)* no coincidence. Playing ____________ *(powerful)* music in the car can lead people to drive more ____________ *(dangerous)* than they otherwise would. In traffic jams, rock music with a ____________ *(heavy)* bass makes us want to move forward ____________ *(fast)*, but since this is not ____________ *(possible)*, we become ____________ *(angry)* and ____________ *(frustrated)*. Being surrounded by rock or dance music in a place where your movements are ____________ *(severe)* restricted, as they are in a car, ____________ *(unfortunate)* tends to block out the part of the brain that ____________ *(normal)* deals with ____________ *(logical)* reasoning. Radio disc jockeys are ____________ *(conscious)* of the ____________ *(psychological)* effect of music on drivers in ____________ *(heavy)* traffic. But they ____________ *(usual)* argue that ____________ *(slow)* or ____________ *(sad)* music only makes people drive too ____________ *(slow)*! In the Netherlands, where road rage is also something that confronts motorists ____________ *(daily)*, the ____________ *(whole)* problem is taken very ____________ *(serious)*. There is a new CD of ____________ *(true)* ____________ *(calming)* music, whose title can be translated as "____________ *(easy)* Driver".

(adapted from *The Times*)

b) Complete this short text with suitable adverbs. Use the adverb forms of these adjectives. There may sometimes be more than one solution.

aggressive angry basic different direct early immediate impatient long normal quick unfortunate usual

There are ____________ two types of "road rage drivers". The first are the people who ____________ behave ____________ and ____________ in everyday situations anyway. So it doesn't take ____________ to make them angry on the road. The second are those who are ____________ calm and peaceful but ____________ react very ____________ on the road. If another driver reacts ____________ to something you have done, you are advised not to look at the other driver ____________, and if possible to drive away ____________. If you are trapped, you should ____________ lock your doors. Recognizing a danger as ____________ as possible is essential.

2 Calvin and school ■ 47

Which form is correct?

fair fairly hard hardly just justly late lately pretty prettily

1. Calvin hasn't been working very ______________ this school year. So his teacher has been complaining a lot ______________.
2. His grade in the last Math test was ______________ poor. No wonder! He ______________ prepared for it at all.
3. A couple of days ago he got to school half an hour ______________. "When I got to the bus stop, the school bus was ______________ disappearing round the corner," he said. "It wasn't my fault!"
4. He's ______________ good at sports, but unfortunately he doesn't always play ______________. So the decision to drop him from the junior basketball team was probably ______________ made.
5. He likes a girl in his grade called Susie. She doesn't really dress very ______________, and they shout at each other a lot, but he always sends her a Valentine.

⁂ 3 Spurs v United (47) ■ 47

Translate this text into English.

[Die] Spurs haben wochenlang sehr hart trainiert. Aber trotzdem werden sie am Samstag wohl kaum eine Chance gegen United haben. Sie haben [zwar] eine Reihe ziemlich guter Spieler und sind hoch motiviert, aber die meisten United Stars sind Weltklasse. Und [schließlich] haben sie gerade [eben] das Endspiel der Champions League gewonnen. Aber in letzter Zeit haben sich auch [die] Spurs verbessert, und besonders die zweite Halbzeit *(half)* im letzten Auswärtsspiel *(away match)* war wirklich ziemlich beeindruckend.

Zu dumm *(too bad)*, dass Tony Richards nicht wird spielen können. Ein Spieler, der die ganze Saison äußerst fair gespielt hat, sah im letzten Heimspiel *(home match)* plötzlich rot – und wurde zu Recht vom Platz gestellt *(to send s.o. off the field)*. Er hatte versucht, Liverpools John Adams zu stoppen, aber unfair und viel zu spät. Diese unfaire Attacke *(tackling)* ist zu Recht mit einer Sperre *(suspension)* von drei Wochen bestraft worden.

4 Workers of the world – in London ■ 50–57

These people all work at a big sandwich shop in Oxford Street, London.

Put the parts of the sentences together. Be careful with the word order!

1. Enza, 29, from Italy:

I / *18 months ago* / *to London* / *came*
quickly / *adapted* / *in London* / *I* / *to life* / *luckily*
always / *in London* / *has* / *my English boyfriend* / *here* / *lived*

2. Vanessa, 22, from Spain:

life / *very hard* / *unfortunately* / *is* / *for me* / *here*
I / *at a drama school* / *in September* / *a course* / *started*
have to go / *I* / *in the morning* / *to school* / *every day*
here / *I* / *in the afternoon* / *then* / *work* / *always*

3. Sang, 19, from Korea:

here / *settled down* / *quickly* / *I* / *pretty*
already / *have* / *I* / *spent* / *with this company* / *two months*
probably / *next February* / *to Korea* / *again* / *return* / *will* / *I*
will / *again* / *maybe* / *later* / *to Britain* / *come back* / *I*

4. Cliff, 35, British:

from different countries / *here* / *are* / *fully* / *people* / *accepted*
actually / *of our 46 employees* / *are* / *only* / *British* / *nine*

5 Punch and Judy shows ■ 50–57

Decide on the best place to put the adverbs and adverbials in these sentences. There are often several ways to do this.

1. Summer time is Punch and Judy time. *(in Britain / every year / at many seaside towns)*
2. The Codman family started their own family tradition of Punch and Judy shows. *(first / in Llandudno, Wales / in 1860)*
3. Jackie Codman and her husband Morris carry it on. *(today / still / amazingly / in the same place)*
4. They use the puppets made by Jackie's great-grandfather, Richard Codman. *(originally / still / all those years ago)*
5. Jackie spends the winter months making new dresses for the puppets and repainting their faces. *(busily / often / carefully)*
6. They perform four 45-minute shows. *(daily / in a space not much bigger than a telephone box)*
7. They are proud of the family tradition. *(very / naturally)*
8. Londoners were the first to see a Punch puppet show. *(in 1622 / actually / however / in Britain / ever)*
9. Punch's birthday is celebrated. *(in the grounds of St Paul's Church, Covent Garden / every year / still / on March 14th)*

6 Links between violent games and aggressive behaviour? ■ 55, 148

Add the given adverbs of comment and linking adverbs to the text to make it sound more interesting.

Playing violent video games is more harmful than watching violence on	*apparently*
TV. Interactive computer games require players to identify with the	
characters carrying out the violence – they increase aggressive thoughts	*so obviously*
and behaviour. A recent scientific study found that students who played	*moreover*
the most computer games did worst at college. Not every child that plays	*of course*
computer games becomes aggressive. But young men who are habitually	*not surprisingly*
aggressive are more vulnerable to the effects of violent games.	
Even a short exposure to video games can increase aggressive behaviour.	*in fact*
Playing a violent video game appears to encourage violent thoughts.	*in the short run*
There aren't any reliable statistics about long term effects. This medium	*though yet*
is more dangerous than violent television and movies.	*probably*
The producers of these games say that there is no link between violent	*not surprisingly clearly*
games and aggressive behaviour. They claim that most video games	*in fact*
contain little or no violence. And it is the parents' job to make sure	*in the end*
that their kids play the right games. There are many critics that demand	*nevertheless actually*
that the industry should stop producing these games altogether.	
Their children might be affected too.	*after all of course*

⁂ 7 A few days in Ireland ■ 50–57

Translate the text into English, paying particular attention to the position of the adverbs and adverbials.

1. Wir versuchen mindestens einmal im Jahr nach England zu fahren. Letztes Jahr waren wir jedoch nicht in England sondern in Wales. Von dort sind wir mit der Fähre für ein paar Tage nach Irland gefahren. Wir sind etwa um vier Uhr nachmittags in Dublin angekommen.
2. Die ersten zwei Tage wollten wir in der Republik Irland bleiben und dann nach Nordirland weiterfahren. Auf den schmalen Straßen in Irland kann man nicht schnell fahren. Die Landschaft ist jedoch so unglaublich schön, dass man eigentlich nie schnell fahren möchte.
3. Überraschenderweise war das Wetter in Irland die ganze Zeit wunderschön.
4. Am zweiten Abend waren wir in einem kleinen Ort an der Grenze zwischen der Republik und Nordirland. Als wir zu unseren Zimmern im zweiten Stock hinaufgingen, kam der Wirt *(landlord)* aus dem Pub im Erdgeschoss und fragte uns, ob wir [nicht] zu einem Glas Guinness herunterkommen wollten.
5. An diesem Abend spielte gerade eine irische Band in dem Pub. Sie spielten außerordentlich gut, und wir kamen leicht mit den anderen Gästen im Pub ins Gespräch *(to get into conversation)*. Das war sicher eines der besten Erlebnisse, die ich je im Urlaub gehabt habe.
6. Leider mussten wir am nächsten Morgen [schon] um sieben Uhr aufstehen und weiterfahren.

Chapter 9 The tenses of the verb

1 The encounter ■ 58, 59

Fill in the simple present or the present progressive. Use the progressive form wherever possible.

Six o'clock. Johnny McDermott, former special agent, now private detective, is just leaving *(just – leave)* his office. He ______ *(usually – leave)* at this time of day. He ______ *(shut)* the door behind him, ______ *(run)* down the stairs from the third floor and ______ *(go out)* into the street. Outside it ______ *(rain)*. Normally Johnny ______ *(walk)* the few blocks to his favourite bar. But the rain ______ *(get)* heavier now. So he ______ *(decide)* to take a cab. Traffic ______ *(move)* very slowly. But at last a cab ______ *(stop)*. He ______ *(get in)* and ______ *(tell)* the driver where to go. When they ______ *(get)* to the bar, Johnny ______ *(see)* a man near the entrance. He ______ *(look)* familiar, although he ______ *(stand)* with his back to Johnny. For a moment Johnny ______ *(not know)* who he ______ *(be)*. Then he ______ *(remember)*. "Razor Charlie! How on earth did he get out of jail?" Johnny ______ *(wonder)*. "______ he ______ *(wait)* for me?" Suddenly the man ______ *(turn)* round. There ______ *(be)* something in his hand, it ______ *(glitter)* in the lights of the cars that ______ *(drive)* past.

2 Which is correct? ■ 58, 59

Underline the correct form.

1. What *(do you do/are you doing)* in your free time? – I *(read/ am reading)* a lot. At the moment I *(read/ am reading)* a book by John Grisham.
2. What a stupid film! I *(don't enjoy/am not enjoying)* it at all. – I *(think/ am thinking)* you *(are/are being)* too critical.
3. Let's switch the light on. It *(gets/is getting)* quite dark already. At this time of the year it *(gets/is getting)* dark so early, *(doesn't/isn't)* it?
4. I *(begin/am beginning)* to get quite cross with Sam. He *(always takes/is always taking)* my things without asking! If I *(ever want/am ever wanting)* to borrow anything of his, I *(always ask/am always asking)* him first.

⁂ 3 Her holiday job ■ 58, 59

Translate the text into English.

„Was machst du die ganze Zeit, Christine? Ich sehe dich nie in der Stadt."
„Ich hab' diesen Ferienjob. Ich arbeite im Augenblick und will etwas Geld verdienen. Ich bin [doch] dabei den Führerschein zu machen *(take driving lessons)*. Und das kostet 'ne Menge Geld. Aber manche Leute haben eben *(just)* reiche Eltern."
„Sehr witzig. Im Übrigen *(by the way)* arbeite ich auch. Ich mache gerade diesen Intensivkurs *(intensive course)* in Englisch, vier Stunden am Tag, ganz schön hart. Aber ich glaube, dass ich langsam besser werde. Du weißt [ja], was für Noten ich in Englisch habe. Und was machst **du** eigentlich genau? Wo arbeitest du?"
„Ich arbeite im Pub am Bahnhof. Es macht mir großen Spaß *(to enjoy s.th.)* – zumindest im Moment. Der Pub öffnet erst am Mittag, so dass ich nicht so früh aufstehen muss. Aber er schließt erst um Mitternacht. Ich treffe immer 'ne Menge interessante Leute. Manchmal kommen auch ein paar Amerikaner in den Pub. Aber so viel Englisch wie du in deinem Intensivkurs lerne ich natürlich nicht. – Oh, es wird spät, ich muss jetzt gehen. Tschüs, Markus."

4 At Heathrow Airport ■ 58, 60, 61

Explain the situation, using the present perfect. Be careful to choose the right form (simple or progressive).

1. A businessman looks annoyed. His flight leaves at 14.10, but he is only just arriving at the airport – at half past two. *(miss)*
   He has missed his flight.
2. Two girls are sitting together in one of the lounges. They arrived at the airport at ten o'clock, and now it is 12.30. *(wait)*
3. There is something wrong with the computer at one of the check-in desks. *(break down)*
4. The tall man checking passports looks tired. He started work seven hours ago. *(work)*
5. A young woman is looking at the menu in one of the restaurants. *(not order – yet)*
6. Two large cases are in a corner near the toilets. Someone left them there several hours ago. *(be)*
7. A woman waiting to go through passport control is looking in all the pockets of her hand luggage. *(forget)*
8. The plane to Amsterdam still can't start because of engine trouble. The passengers got on the plane over an hour ago. *(sit)*

5 *Since* or *for*? ■ 58, 60, 61

Translate these sentences into English. Use the progressive form wherever possible.

1. Ich freue mich schon ewig auf diesen Film!
2. Er läuft *(to be on)* erst seit Mittwoch.
3. Ich war schon seit Wochen nicht [mehr] im Kino.
4. Seit meinem Geburtstag habe ich keinen wirklich guten Film [mehr] gesehen.
5. Sarah arbeitet seit zwei Jahren für die BBC in London.
6. Johns neue Freundin ist Schauspielerin. Sie kennen sich schon seit ein paar Monaten.
7. Gehen wir ein bisschen nach draußen. Wir sitzen schon stundenlang vor dem Fernseher!

6 Scared to death ■ 58, 62

Two teenage girls wrote to a magazine about the times they felt most scared.

Choose between the simple and the progressive form of the past tense. Use the progressive form wherever possible.

1. "It ________________ *(happen)* a few years ago. My brother and I ________________ *(play)* in the park. We ________________ *(have)* his go-kart with us, and I ________________ *(persuade)* him to let me ride it down the steep hill there. I ________________ *(get)* on and ________________ *(ride)* off, but after a few moments I ________________ *(realize)* that the go-kart ________________ *(get)* faster and faster – and I ________________ *(not know)* how to stop it! There ________________ *(be)* a busy main road at the bottom of the hill, and the traffic on it ________________ *(move)* fast. When I ________________ *(see)* it, I ________________ *(think)*: 'This is it, I'm going to die!' At the last moment, as the go-kart ________________ *(race)* through the big park gates, a miracle ________________ *(happen)*. The traffic lights ________________ *(change)*, and all the cars ________________ *(stop)*, and the go-kart just ________________ *(sail)* through the middle." *(Nina, Liverpool)*

2. "I ________________ *(look)* after my two younger sisters one day when our mum ____________ *(be)* out. We ________________ *(eat)* nuts when suddenly Jodie, my youngest sister, ________________ *(swallow*[1]*)* a whole nut and ________________ *(start)* to choke[2]. It ________________ *(be)* awful. She ________________ *(get)* blue in the face, and my other sister ________________ *(shout)* at me to do something. I ________________ *(know)* there ________________ *(be)* no time to call an ambulance. So I ________________ *(pick)* Jodie up by her ankle[3] and ________________ *(hold)* her upside down. Then, while I ________________ *(hold)* her like that, I ________________ *(hit)* her on the back, really hard, until the nut ________________ *(come)* shooting out. When Mum ________________ *(get)* home, the three of us ________________ *(sit)* there in floods of tears. I ________________ *(cry)* from shock, and my sisters because I had hit Jodie so hard on the back!"

(Melanie, Solihull)

[1] **to swallow** *schlucken* – [2] **to choke** *ersticken* – [3] **ankle** *Knöchel*

(adapted from *SHOUT* magazine)

7 Travelling ■ 60–63

Complete the sentences with the right verb form (past tense or present perfect, simple or progressive).

1. Let's stop for our picnic soon. We ________________ *(sit)* in the car for hours!
2. My brother ________________ *(have)* a holiday in Canada last summer.
3. ________ the Camerons ________________ *(come)* back from Spain yet? – No, they ________________.
4. ________ you ________________ *(have)* good weather when you ________________ *(be)* in Scotland? – No, I ________________ *(never – know)* it so cold. While we ________________ *(stay)* in Fort William, it even ________________ *(start)* snowing!
5. I ________________ *(not – see)* your holiday photos yet.
6. ________ Melanie ________________ *(ring up)* since she ________________ *(go)* off on that trip with Lucy?
7. Dad ________________ *(wait)* for us at the airport when we ________________ *(get)* back from Thailand.
8. ________ you ________________ *(write)* a card to Robin? – Yes, I ________________ *(send)* it off yesterday.
9. One of my uncles ________________ *(live)* in Toronto for years now, but we ________________ *(not – visit)* him so far.
10. ________ you ________________ *(visit)* the Fosters when you ________________ *(go)* down to Cornwall last summer? – No, we ________________ *(not – have)* time.

⁂ 8 Australia – nation of colonies ■ 63, 78

Past tense or present perfect? Use the simple forms only in this text.
(Sometimes passive forms will be needed.)

European settlement of Australia ______________ *(begin)* in 1788, when a British penal[1] colony ______________ *(found)* on the east coast, at a place which since then ______________ *(develop)* into the great city of Sydney. All in all, six colonies ______________ *(eventually – establish)* in Australia, but it ______________ *(not – be)* until 1901 that they ______________ *(all – join)* together as a federation. Before that year, each area ______________ *(have)* its own system of taxes and laws; there ______________ *(even – be)* different postage stamps for the different colonies!

Since January 1st 1901, Australia ______________ *(be)* one nation. But even today, differences between the individual states ______________ *(not yet – disappear)* entirely. Although the borders between the states ______________ *(all – abolish)*, the fact that each state issues its own driving licence ______________ *(not – change)* so far. Trains ______________ *(only – be able to)* travel from one state to another since the 1980s; before that this ______________ *(not – be)* possible because the width of the tracks ______________ *(vary)* from state to state.

When the new nation ______________ *(declare)* in 1901, it ______________ *(need)* a capital. Rivalry between the two biggest cities in New South Wales and Victoria, Sydney and Melbourne, ______________ *(be)* so great that it ______________ *(eventually – agree)* to build a new city as a capital somewhere in the bush. But although Canberra ______________ *(since then – become)* one of the nation's largest cities, it ______________ *(never – be able to)* match the other Australian cities for flair. It ______________ *(remain)* a quiet city of parks, trees, plazas – and government buildings.

[1] **penal** *Straf-*

9 Wyatt Earp ■ 64

Wyatt Earp was one of the most famous heroes in the Wild West.

Connect the two sentences with the help of the given conjunctions, using the simple past perfect in one of the clauses.

1. The Earp family first lived in Monmouth, Illinois. In 1864 the family moved to California. *(before)*
   Before the Earp family moved to California in 1864, they had lived in Monmouth, Illinois.
2. Young Wyatt Earp travelled all over the country. Then he started to work on the construction of the Union Pacific Railway. *(after)*
3. In Illinois he served as a deputy and marshal for several towns. His wanderings finally led him to Tombstone. *(after)*
4. Wild Bill Hickock taught him how to shoot in Kansas City. But Wyatt preferred to settle fights without the aid of firearms. *(although)*
5. Wyatt arrived in Tombstone in the fall of 1879. He was appointed deputy sheriff of this wild and dangerous place. *(soon after)*
6. Wyatt Earp succeeded in reducing crime in Tombstone. The Clanton Gang "ran" the town before that. *(before)*
7. Wyatt Earp's activities began to affect their "business interests". So "Old Man" Clanton decided to kill the sheriff. *(because)*
8. Wyatt Earp was warned to keep away from the Clantons and their followers. But he and his friend Doc Holliday went to meet them at the OK Corral. *(although)*
9. The dust settled after a 30-second shootout. Two of the Clantons were dead, and one was badly wounded. *(when)*
10. But the Clantons took their revenge and shot two of Wyatt's brothers. Wyatt got tired of fighting and left Tombstone. *(when)*

⁂ 10 Why Charles I lost his head ■ 64, 78

Decide which forms of the given verbs to use – simple past, simple past perfect or past perfect progressive. (Sometimes you'll have to use passive forms too.)

When Elizabeth I ______________ *(die)* in 1603, she ______________ *(be)* on the throne for 45 years. As she ______________ *(have)* no children, the crown ______________ *(pass)* to her cousin, James Stuart. James ______________ *(be)* King of Scotland since he ______________ *(be)* a baby. He now ______________ *(become)* the first person to rule both countries. After his death in 1625, his son Charles I ______________ *(succeed)* him.

For centuries Parliament and the Monarch ______________ *(argue)* about which of the two ______________ *(be)* more powerful. Charles ______________ *(believe)* in the "Divine Right of Kings". He ______________ *(teach)* by his father that kings ______________ *(appoint)* by God and that the people ______________ *(have to)* obey the king. After he ______________ *(rule)* the country without Parliament for 11 years, Charles ______________ *(have to)* call Parliament because he ______________ *(need)* money for his family and for war with Scotland. It ______________ *(always – be)* Parliament's right to raise taxes. After Charles ______________ *(listen)* to the complaints of the MPs for days, he ______________ *(lose)* patience and ______________ *(send)* them away. But soon after, he ______________ *(have to)* call them again because his army ________ *(beat)* by the Scots and Charles ________ *(promise)* to pay money to the victorious army.

When Parliament ________ *(demand)* that Charles should share command of a new army with the MPs, he ________ *(believe)* they ________ *(want)* to take all his power. He ________ *(storm)* into Parliament with his soldiers, wanting to arrest five leading MPs. But they ________ *(warn)* beforehand and ________ *(escape)*. When Parliament now ________ *(start)* to pass laws that the King ________ *(not agree to)*, he ________ *(raise)* an army.

Parliament ________ *(raise)* an army, too. War ________ *(begin)*. The Royalists and the Parliamentarians ________ *(fight)* for six years, when finally the King ________ *(capture)* in 1648. After he ________ *(try*[1]*)* in court and ________ *(find)* guilty, he ________ *(execute)* in 1649. The trial and execution of the King by his own subjects ________ *(be)* something that ________ *(never – happen)* in England before. But Parliament ________ *(win)* the struggle.

[1] **to try** *vor Gericht stellen*

11 What is going to happen? ■ 66

Use the going-to-future to say what the people in these situations are going to do and what is going to happen. The verbs on the right will help you.
Put a "(p)" after the sentences that express a plan or intention and a "(c)" after the ones that express that something is certain to happen.

be late cut off fall have (frightful crash) play put on ✔ rain sink steal win

1. She is going to put on her glasses. (p)

12 Spontaneous decisions ■ 68

Use the will-*future and the given words to react to these sentences.*

1. Phew, it's hot in here. – ... *(window)* I'll open the window.
2. Which are you going to have, tea or coffee? – ... *(tea)*
3. This exercise is rather difficult. – ... *(show)*
4. I've forgotten my pen. – ... *(lend)*
5. Oh dear, look at that pile of dirty dishes. – ... *(washing-up)*
6. I hope you'll enjoy your holidays in Ireland. – ... *(postcard)*
7. Oh, I haven't got any more stamps. – ... *(get)*
8. It's a secret, remember! – ... *(not tell)*

13 Plans and their results ■ 66, 68

What are these people thinking? Say what they are going to do and what will happen as a result. Choose from these expressions:

have hair cut✓ learn words look better✓ buy this one get really good taste great go with new skirt have lots of time in town add more wine practise hard do well in test take early train

1.

1. I'm going to have my hair cut. Then it'll look better!

2. ______ →

2.

3.

3. ______

4. ______ →

4.

5.

5. ______

6. ______ →

6.

14 Ranger programs ■ 69

Activity	Time/Place
Native American Lifestyle Learn about Native American life (lifeways, family relationships, language, songs).	11:00 a.m. Mon. Visitor Center
Fire on the Rim Discover fire managing techniques with a ranger and a firefighter.	11:00 p.m. Tue. Yaki Point
On the Edge Leisurely rim walk – perspective of Grand Canyon and its cultural and natural history	1:30 p.m. Wed. El Torva Hotel
Campfire Talk Relax and enjoy an hour by the campfire with a ranger: stories, sing-alongs. Dress warmly.	8:00 p.m. Thurs. Sage Loop Campfire Circle
Pleasures of a Starry Sky Explore the Milky Way and other wonders of the night sky.	9:00 p.m. Fri. Mather Point
The Spirit of Sunset Peace, tradition, mystery. Come watch the ever-changing colors of sunset as we explore one of the Canyon's many secrets.	60 min. before sunset Sat. Desert View Point

Tom is a ranger at the Grand Canyon. He is talking to a visitor about some of his jobs during the next week.

Write down what Tom is saying, using the future progressive of these verbs.

talk about explain about show look at *take for a walk* *tell stories and sing songs*

On Monday morning I'll be talking about Native American life.
On Tuesday morning I'll be …

15 Arrangements and predictions ■ 67, 68, 70

Answer these questions, using the will*-future, the present progressive or the simple present with these expressions:*

go to – America collect – at half past seven go to – McDonalds play – start – 8 p.m. *be – sunny in the morning – wet later* *be – 75 – next month train – leave – 9.20 stay with – grandfather in Chicago*

1. What are your plans for the summer holidays? – ______________________.
   – Where exactly? – ______________________.
   – How old is your grandfather? – ______________________.
2. Have you seen the weather forecast? – ______________________.
3. When must you be at the station? – ______________________.
4. Do you know when we'll have to be at the theatre? – ______________________.
   – And what about Carol? How will she get there? – ______________________.
   – And after the performance? Have you arranged anything? – ______________________.

16 Invading England ■ 65–72

William of Normandy has been waiting for a favourable wind for almost six weeks. Imagine that he is talking to his army before the invasion. (Let's pretend that he speaks English.)
Underline the most suitable of the given verb forms.

"My friends, we have been waiting a long time now, and I can understand that you're getting impatient. But I'm sure that this long wait (*ends/will end/will have ended*) very soon. As soon as the wind *(is changing/is going to change/changes)*, we (*sail/will have sailed/will sail*) to England. And don't worry about the battle. We *(win/are going to win/are winning)* the day. I'm sure that our superbly trained war-horses (*are frightening /will frighten/frighten*) the English foot-soldiers away. And, very probably, our arrows (*are raining/rain/will rain*) death on them. We (*will not stop/are not stopping/do not stop*) fighting until we (*will be winning/will win/have won*). And I hope, friends, that God (*is going to be/will be/is*) with us.
As soon as we (*are going to win/will win/have won*) the battle, we *(will make for/will have made for/are going to make for*) London. Believe me, friends, in three weeks' time the Londoners (*are welcoming/ welcome/will have welcomed)* us with open arms and we (*are marching/march/will be marching*) into that great city.
I expect there (*is/is going to be/will be*) little resistance. But if there (*is going to be/will be/is*), we (*are building/build/will build)* strong castles. You, my knights, (*are going to be/will have been/are*) the masters of those castles, and the masters of England. And when I (*have been crowned/will be crowned/am going to be crowned*) in Westminster Abbey, I (*am/will have been/will be*) King of England!!! When I (*am going to be/will have been/am)* King, all of you (*are rewarded/have been rewarded/will be rewarded*) richly. And if God (*is going to be/will be/is*) with us, we (*build/are building/will build)* great cathedrals to thank Him.

⁂ 17 German *Präsens* in English ■ 59, 60, 65–71

✎ *Decide how best to translate the German* Präsens *in these sentences: simple present, present progressive, simple present perfect, present perfect progressive,* going-to-*future or* will-*future?*

1. Wenn der Bus nicht bald kommt, verpassen wir unseren Zug.
2. Unser Zug fährt um 10.32 ab. – Wann kommt er in Paris an?
3. Hier spricht Ihr Kapitän. Wir fliegen gerade über den Ärmelkanal. Voraussichtlich landen wir in etwa 30 Minuten in London Heathrow.
4. Jetzt kommt unser Gepäck. – Moment, ich hole einen Kofferkuli *(trolley)*.
5. Nächste Woche reisen wir nach Wien. – Wie lange seid ihr dann weg?
6. Meine Damen und Herren, leider haben wir ein Problem mit einem der Triebwerke *(engines)*. Wir machen eine Notlandung *(emergency landing)*.
7. Weißt du, dass Sue jetzt in London lebt? – Ja, das weiß ich schon lange, sie arbeitet [ja] schon seit einiger Zeit für British Airways.
8. Ich rufe dich an, wenn wir in New York ankommen.

*"Hurry up, sir – I'll **tell** you how the film ends."*

18 At Loch Ness ■ 74, 75

Use the present tense sequence to describe the situation. The following words and phrases will help you.

sunny afternoon – August   Mr and Mrs Brown – enjoy – holiday – Scotland   leave home – three days ago – travel – Edinburgh – where – spend – couple of nights   now – arrive – Loch Ness   of course – both – hear of – Loch Ness Monster – so – hope – monster – appear – while – there   twenty minutes ago – park – car – edge of loch – Mr Brown – get – camera – ready – both – sit down – grass   but – not see – monster – yet   Mrs Brown – get – bored – both – begin – feel hungry   now – wait – for quite a long time – but – Mr Brown – not give up – hope – yet   think – perhaps – still – see – monster   if – not appear – in the next five minutes – have to – give up – after all

"We'll give it another five minutes."

It's a sunny afternoon in August. Mr and Mrs Brown are enjoying . . .

19 October 1066 ■ 74, 75

Complete the text, keeping to the past tense sequence. Sometimes progressive forms will be needed.

On October 1st 1066, only a few days after he __________ *(beat)* the Norwegians at the Battle of Stamford Bridge in the North of England, Harold __________ *(hear)* that William of Normandy __________ *(land)* on the south coast. Harold and his men __________ *(rest)* at York when the news __________ *(come)*. Although he __________ *(lose)* many of his men at Stamford Bridge and those who __________ *(survive)* the battle __________ *(be)* now tired, Harold __________ *(begin)* the march south on October 3rd. He __________ *(know)* that by the time they __________ *(reach)* the south coast, they __________ *(be)* exhausted, but there __________ *(be)* no alternative. In London, a few reinforcements[1] __________ *(wait)* to join them as soon as they __________ *(reach)* the Thames. By October 13th, the Normans __________ *(be)* in sight. Harold's army __________ *(be)* probably larger than William's, but the Normans __________ *(rest)* for over two weeks, which __________ *(be)* an enormous advantage in the battle next day.

October 14th __________ *(be)* the decisive day. Until late in the afternoon, it __________ *(not be)* clear which side __________ *(win)* the battle. The turning point __________ *(come)* when the English, who up to that moment __________ *(fight)* from a strong position at the top of a hill, __________ *(rush)* down after the Norman soldiers, who __________ *(pretend)* to run away. When the Normans __________ *(see)* that the English __________ *(abandon)* their position of strength, they __________ *(turn)* back and __________ *(start)* fighting again. Then Harold __________ *(be hit)* by an arrow – in the eye. When the English

[1] **reinforcements** extra troops

__________ *(hear)* that he and two of his brothers __________ *(be killed)*, they __________ *(give up)* the fight, and the Normans __________ *(win)* the day. If Harold and his men __________ *(beat)* William's army on that autumn day, the future of England __________ *(be)* very different.

20 Be a green visitor ■ 75

The South West of England is popular for walking and cycling. Visitors to the area are asked to be as "green" as they can.

✎ *Why are these country rules important? What will or may happen if people don't keep to them? Make logical sentences. (You may find these words and phrases useful, but you can use your own ideas, too.)*

Country rules
1. Do not disturb livestock.[1]
2. Keep your dog under close control.
3. Fasten all gates properly behind you.
4. Do not leave litter – take it home with you.
5. Do not disturb wild animals or birds.
6. Leave farm crops and machines alone.
7. Keep to public footpaths across farmland.
8. Take special care on country roads.

[1] **livestock** farm animals

chase sheep cows attack be frightened escape spoil countryside run road crops cause damage accident farmer get annoyed catch fire

1. If you disturb livestock, the animals will be frightened. Or they may even attack you.

21 No problem! ■ 75

Kirsty works for the "Problem Page" of GLAM magazine.
✎ *What advice does she give to these people? Choose from the ideas on the right.*

1. I make so many spelling mistakes in tests!
   You wouldn't make so many mistakes if you read your work through carefully before you handed it in.
2. I never have time for a proper breakfast!
3. I get so bored at the weekends!
4. I always get through my pocket money so quickly!
5. I have trouble choosing things like clothes and make-up!
6. My mum complains so much about the mess in my room!
7. I never remember my friends' birthdays!

Write them in your diary.
Tidy up regularly.
Take a friend with you to the shops!
Plan your spending carefully.
Get up twenty minutes earlier.
Read your work through carefully before you hand it in. ✓
Go out with friends – or join a club.

22 How a rainy day can bring you luck ■ 75

Here's how my mum met my dad – all those years ago ...
My mum was in town one day and it started raining, so she went into a café and had a cup of tea. She picked up a magazine lying on the table and looked through it. She saw there was a competition on the back page. It still hadn't stopped raining, so she stayed in the café, read all the quiz questions and wrote in the answers. The prizes sounded good, so she decided to take part in the competition.
A month or so later, she heard that she'd won a prize – a ticket for Wimbledon! My mum has always loved watching tennis – so she went to Wimbledon, of course. While she was watching a match on the Centre Court, it started to rain. She had forgotten to bring her umbrella, but the young man in the seat next to hers shared his umbrella with her – and they got into conversation ... And that was how they got to know each other!

✎ *Look at the text carefully. Use sentences with* if *to show how one thing led to another. Make at least five sensible sentences.*

If it hadn't started raining that day, she would never have gone into that café and had a cup of tea.
If she hadn't ...

23 If things were (or had been) different ■ 75

Make sentences with **if** *to sum up the following situations.*

1. We can't possibly visit any of the other solar systems. They're all so far away!
   If the other solar systems weren't so far away, we would/might possibly be able to visit some of them.
2. They have a dog – so going abroad for holidays is a problem.
3. We arrived late because we took the wrong exit off the motorway.
4. My father didn't learn Latin at school, so he can't help me with my homework.
5. I didn't buy that T-shirt – it was so expensive!
6. Simon didn't have to get up early in the holidays because he didn't do a paper round after all.
7. I'm not wearing my glasses, so I can't read that sign over there.
8. We have relations in London, so we didn't stay at a hotel.
9. I didn't collect you at the station, but you never asked me to!
10. Ben is allowed to have the car tonight. Mum doesn't need it.

24 Possible problems – possible solutions ■ 76

Suggest solutions to the people with these fears. Use **should** *after* **if**, *and then make suggestions with* **will/would be able to** *or* **can/could always**.

1. Maybe I'll miss my train.
   – If you should miss your train, you'll be able to take the next one.
2. You may be out when I phone.
3. The tickets will probably be all sold out.
4. Perhaps Sue won't like the CD I've bought her.
5. I bet it'll rain when we have the barbecue!
6. The station car park is sure to be full!

leave a message
change it
take the next one ✓
try the one behind the post office
go to another show instead
use the grill in the kitchen

25 On the beach ■ 77

What are they thinking? Make sentences with I wish …, If only … I'd rather …. *These ideas will help you:*

"Wouldn't it be easier to go back and get your reading glasses?"

remember – reading glasses
not interfere
go back – get glasses
not be – so forgetful
behave – more sensibly
not be – so critical
be able – read without glasses
not be – such a long walk back to hotel

He: I wish I was able to read without glasses.

Chapter 10 The passive voice

1 The worst floods for 40 years ■ 78, 79

Put the active constructions (marked) into the passive. Decide whether you think a by*-agent should be used.*

The worst floods for 40 years have hit the South East of England. Yesterday, as rivers in Kent burst their banks, **the Army had to rescue hundreds of people from their homes. Water has flooded some low-lying areas** twice already this year. In parts of Sussex, as the water is beginning to subside[1], **farmers have discovered a number of drowned sheep and cattle. The flooding has totally destroyed many farmers' land and herds.** Some say **it could ruin them.**
In Maidstone, Kent, **high tides swelled the River Medway**. Throughout the morning, **the council delivered hundreds of sandbags.** In Yalding **the fire brigade rescued 32 adults and 15 children from their homes.** Angela Shave, 45, said, "My husband and I were trapped upstairs with the water level still rising. We were afraid **the water would sweep us away**."
In order to avoid future problems, **the government is to restrict building on river banks and flood plains.** Local authorities will normally no longer allow new homes on at-risk sites. The policy's first test will probably be at Ashford, Kent, where **the local council has already passed plans for thousands of new homes near the river Stour.** A spokesman for the Environment Agency said, "We hope **they will build the Ashford homes on higher, safer ground**." Unfortunately, builders prefer to construct on flood plains; because the land there is flat, **they can develop it more cheaply.**

(based on articles in *The Times*)

[1] **to subside** *zurückgehen, sinken*

2 The £25 million spaniel ■ 78, 79

Scooby's amazing drugs haul[1]

When Scooby, the Spaniel **was abandoned** at the age of two, his future looked uncertain. He **had been left** at a dogs' home in Devon and, if an owner **had not been found**, he **would have been put down**[2].
Yet today he **is valued** by his grateful owners at an astonishing £25 million. Scooby is one of Britain's most successful sniffer dogs – and £25 million is the street value of the drugs that **have been uncovered** by him in the last four years. So important is the work done at the port of Dover by Scooby and his fellow Customs and Excise[3] dogs that they **will be taken** to the Crofts Dog Show next week – as guests of honour.
All the dogs **have** either **been donated** by members of the public or **taken** from animal rescue centres. Nigel Knott of Customs and Excise explained how the dogs **are trained**.
"In training, toy items **are produced** and the dog **is teased** with them," he said. "They **are hidden** in increasingly inaccessible[4] places and the odours[5] of the drugs **are** gradually **impregnated** into them. In time, the dog responds to the smells, mostly heroin, cocaine and cannabis."
Now aged seven, Scooby will retire and, after the show next week, **will be given** to his handler, Jenny Wood.
Without any doubt, his retirement **has been** well **earned.**

(adapted from the *Daily Mail*)

[1] **haul** a large amount of goods that has been stolen, or found by the police – [2] **to put down** to kill an animal by putting it to sleep – [3] **(Board of) Customs and Excise** *Zollbehörde* – [4] **inaccessible** impossible or very difficult to reach – [5] **odour** (unpleasant) smell

Use active verb forms to answer these questions.

1. What did Scooby's owners do when he was two years old?
2. What did they almost do to him at the dogs' home?
3. What do his owners think of him today?
4. How has Scooby become so valuable?
5. How will the Customs and Excise people show that they are proud of Scooby and the other dogs?
6. How did Scooby and the others become Customs and Excise dogs?
7. Explain how the dog handlers train the dogs.
8. What will happen to Scooby after his retirement?

3 Fatal shark attacks in Australia ■ 78, 79

Translate the text into English.

Gestern ist in Australien ein 49-jähriger Schwimmer von einem Hai getötet worden. Das Unglück *(fatal accident)* ereignete sich unweit *(not far from)* des beliebten Cottlesloe-Strandes nahe der Stadt Perth. Nachdem er aus dem Wasser gezogen worden war, starb der Mann. Sein linkes Bein war abgebissen worden. Ein Freund, der das Opfer *(victim)* an Land schleppte *(to drag)*, wurde an Beinen und Füßen gebissen und musste ins Krankenhaus gebracht werden. Die Strände von Perth wurden nach dem Unglück gesperrt *(to close)*.
Innerhalb von *(in the space of)* nur sechs Wochen sind jetzt drei Männer Opfer von Haien in Australien geworden. Ende September wurde bei Adelaide ein Surfer von einem weißen Hai *(great white shark)* getötet. Der 25-jährige Hochzeitsreisende *(honeymooner)* aus Neuseeland war nur 50 Meter vom Ufer entfernt *(away from the shore)* von seinem Surfbrett in die Tiefe gerissen worden *(to pull s.o. into the depths of the sea)*. Sein Brett wurde später gefunden, von seiner Leiche *(body)* aber fehlte jede Spur *(to disappear without a trace)*.
Einen Tag nachdem der neuseeländische Tourist getötet worden war, starb ein 17-jähriger Surfer bei Elliston, 450 Kilometer westlich von Adelaide; er wurde ebenfalls von einem Hai angegriffen und getötet.

INFO: Im Schnitt *(on average)* wird pro Jahr weniger als eine tödliche *(fatal)* Hai-Attacke verzeichnet *(to register)*.

(based on articles in the *Südwest Presse*)

4 Hadrian's Wall ■ 78, 79

Complete the text with the correct passive forms of the given verbs. (You will also have to use some non-finite forms.)

Lost stretch of Hadrian's Wall discovered

A long-lost section of Hadrian's Wall ____________________ (*discover*) in Newcastle-upon-Tyne. The foundations ____________________ (*find*) during construction of a public leisure centre. Paul Bidell, head of archaeology at Tyne and Wear Museum, said that 20 yards of the foundations ____________________ (*restore*) in the near future. "At the moment the first short stretch ____________________ (*dig up*)," he said.

Emperor Hadrian ordered the Wall ____________________ (*build*) in 122. In the early 1990s, at *Vindolanda*, a large palace of some 50 rooms ____________________ (*discover*). Recently it ____________________ (*date*) to about AD 120, and therefore it ____________________ (*believe*) to be the headquarters from which the construction of the Wall ____________________ (*supervise*) by the Emperor himself.

The Wall is the most important monument ____________________ (*build*) by the Romans in Britain, and it is the best-known frontier in the entire Roman empire. When Hadrian's Wall ____________________ (*complete*), it ran for 117 kilometres, from the North Sea to the Irish Sea.

The construction of the Wall ____________________ (*carry out*) by the three Roman legions in the province. (The idea that the Wall ____________________ (*build*) by slave labour is wrong.) And modifications ____________ still ____________________ (*make*) at the time of Hadrian's death in 138.

The province ______________________ (*protect*) from the "barbarians" in the North and the frontier ______________________ (*control*). The Wall ______________________ (*guard*) by soldiers from the Northern provinces, not by soldiers from Rome or Italy. Each of the forts on the Wall appears to ______________________ (*build*) to hold a regiment of soldiers.

After the legions ______________________ (*order*) back to defend Rome at the beginning of the 5th century, the Wall ______________________ (*leave*) to decay. In the Middle Ages, the Wall ____________ frequently ________________ (*plunder*) for stones, which ______________________ (*use*) to build houses and churches.

Today the Wall ______________________ (*look after*) by *English Heritage* and ______________________ (*visit*) by thousands of tourists every year.

5 Crime and other problems ■ 79, 80

✎ *Put these sentences into the passive, being careful with the prepositions. Use a* by-*agent only when you feel it is needed.*

1. I think we can really rely on our local police.
   I think our local police can really be relied on.
2. Burglars broke into the Hunters' house while they were away on holiday.
3. They broke a window, but I imagine the insurance will pay for that.
4. I think the law should deal with hooligans more strictly.
5. The Palmers last saw their son three weeks ago, and nobody has heard of him since.
6. There wouldn't be so many dogs in animal rescue centres if their owners looked after them properly.
7. People often take unfair advantage of small children and of the elderly.
8. The police are looking into the details of the case very thoroughly.

6 Saying it differently ■ 81

✎ *Change what these people say, using the personal passive. The stress will be slightly different, but the meaning should remain the same.*

1. They gave us free drinks when we arrived.
   We were given free drinks when we arrived.
2. On the first evening of our holiday, they showed us a film about the island.
3. Has anyone ever offered you drugs?
4. Lucky you! Nobody has ever given me a free ticket for a rock concert!
5. How much do they pay you for helping out in the shop? – Not as much as they first promised me!
6. They're going to offer John a part in the play after all.
7. I don't think they'll send us an invitation to the wedding.
8. Those are nice flowers. Yes, someone gave them to me on my birthday.

⁂ 7 What people say ■ 82

✎ *Use* **be believed to**, **be known to**, **be supposed to**, **be said to** *or* **be thought to** *to translate these sentences into English.*

1. Sie soll die älteste Frau der Welt sein.
2. Einige von Shakespeares Sonetten wurden vermutlich von anderen Autoren geschrieben.
3. Politiker versprechen bekanntlich viel.
4. Man nimmt an, dass die Bankräuber im Auto eines Freundes entkommen sind.
5. Man glaubt, dass die Aborigines vor über 60 000 Jahren nach Australien kamen.

1 *Be, have* or *do*? ■ 83–86

Fill in the correct forms of **be**, **have** *or* **do**. *(Sometimes you will have to use combinations of these verbs.)*

1. What ____________ you ____________ at the weekend? Anything interesting?
2. She ____________ her homework since she went up to her room. That ____________ two hours ago.
3. What ____________ Sarah ____________? – She ____________ a bath at the moment.
4. ____________ your brother play football? – No, he ____________, but I ____________.
5. ____________ you ____________ the washing-up yet? – I'm afraid I ____________.
6. The "King's Head" ____________ in the High Street, ____________ it? – Yes, it ____________ there since the Middle Ages.
7. You ____________ talked to me all evening. You ____________ very uncommunicative.
8. ____________ you always ____________ a shower in the morning? – Yes, normally I ____________, but this morning I ____________. I ____________ in too much of a hurry.
9. What ________ we ____________ for lunch today? – Chicken. – Oh, I ____________ love chicken!

"No, you can't have chicken for dinner – we've had it twice already."

2 Reacting to different situations ■ 87, 88

Use modal auxiliaries and the words in brackets to react to these situations.

1. You are out with a friend, but you've forgotten your purse. *Make a request. (lend)*
   Could / Would / Can you lend me some money?
2. Your friend has forgotten to send his grandfather a birthday card. *Make a suggestion. (ring up)*
3. Your father lives quite near his work, but always goes by car, whatever the weather. *Give some advice. (walk)*
4. You are at a friend's house and you need to ring your parents up. *Make a request. (use)*
5. Your aunt takes out a cigarette in a non-smoking area. *Say it's not allowed. (smoke)*
6. You are going to borrow a friend's camera, and you know how to work it. *Say something is unnecessary. (show)*
7. Your sister is always tired in the mornings. *Express a criticism. (stay up)*
8. You and your friend want to take the bus into town, but you leave a bit late. *Say something is possible. (miss)*
9. You are expecting a phone call from Sue. The phone rings. *Say something is certain. (be)*

3 Say it with auxiliaries ■ 87–92

Use auxiliaries to express these ideas in a different way.

can✓ can can't could couldn't may might mustn't needn't

1. It sometimes gets very cold here in the winter.
   It can get very cold here in the winter.
2. I really find it impossible to concentrate.
3. It's wrong to leave a dog locked in a car on a hot day.
4. Would it be possible for you to park somewhere else?
5. I have a feeling this is a short cut, but perhaps I'm wrong.
6. My father is very strict at times.
7. Perhaps the supermarket on Monks Road is still open – it's just possible.
8. The waiter didn't know a word of English.
9. Don't call me back – it's not necessary.

4 Must? Mustn't? Needn't? ■ 91, 92

Which is suitable?

must mustn't needn't

1. I'm not hurt. You ____________ worry.
2. Your parents ____________ have felt terribly worried when you didn't come home.
3. The oven's very hot. Tell Timmy he ____________ touch it.
4. Thanks for the chocolates! But you ____________ have got me a present really.
5. It's a secret. You ____________ tell anyone!
6. We ____________ warn the neighbours about our party. They'll be away.
7. You ____________ come and visit us some time.
8. She ____________ have had a reason for what she did.
9. You ____________ explain. I know all about it already.
10. He easily gets upset. You ____________ say anything to hurt his feelings.

5 Could you be a police officer? ■ 89, 91, 92

Use appropriate forms of **have to, be able to** *and* **be allowed to**.

Could you be a police officer? Do you think you would ________________ deal with all the situations a police officer ________________ deal with in his or her job? Or even if you applied, do you think you ________________ join the police?

Patsy: I've been with the police for five years. In that time I ________________ do a lot of quite difficult things. Yesterday, for example, I ________________ talk to a 15-year-old schoolgirl. Her boyfriend is a drug dealer. I tried to persuade her to shop[1] him, but she felt she *(not)* ________________ do it. I'm going to ________________ talk to her again tomorrow. Of course, she's terrified of what he might do to her. But I still hope I ________________ persuade her.

[1] **to shop s.o.** *jdn. verpfeifen*

Dave: Last Saturday the police ________________ deal with some trouble after a football match. This is always difficult. When the fans get violent, we ________________ try to disperse[2] them calmly. Of course, we *(not)* ________________ use violence ourselves, but we ________________ defend ourselves if it gets really rough. On Saturday things were pretty bad, but we ________________ restore order eventually. Six blokes[3] ________________ be arrested, though.

Diane: What do you think it feels like to ________________ go round to somebody's house and tell a woman that her husband and two children have been killed in a car crash? I ________________ do that last week. At first I thought I *(not)* ________________ do it. I was glad there was another officer with me, so I *(not)* ________________ go alone.

Jack: Each year, about 35,000 people apply for a job with the police, but only about 5,000 ________________ join. You ________________ be very fit, for one thing. If you apply but you aren't fit enough, you *(not)* ________________ join the police. Would you ________________ chase a shoplifter up the stairs of a tower block, for example? ________________ do things like that is vital in the police force. People who *(not)* ________________ pass the medical[4] ________________ be turned down[5]. Of course, there are other qualities we ________________ look out for apart from physical fitness. ________________ observe and remember the details of scenes accurately is very important, for example. A police officer also ________________ ________________ behave sensitively and with compassion towards every man, woman and child he or she meets. People often don't realize how challenging police work is. (based on an article in *The Daily Telegraph*)

[2] **to disperse (a crowd)** *zerstreuen* – [3] **bloke** *Kerl, Typ* – [4] **medical** *Einstellungsuntersuchung* – [5] **to turn s.o. down** *jdn. abweisen*

6 Will you help me, please? ■ 93

Use **will, would** *and other expressions for German* wollen *to finish what these people are saying. (Sometimes there are several possibilities.) Use these ideas:*

dial for me
(not) eat any dog biscuits
(not) give it to me
(always) go there
help me translate it
(not) have my hair cut
live in a warmer country
(not) pay so much
(not) see a doctor
set the table ✔
shut the window
(not) start in cold weather

1. I'm terribly busy in the kitchen and lunch is late anyway. **... you ...?**
   Will you / Would you set the table, please?
2. Our dog only eats leftovers. **He ...**
3. That car costs at least £20,000. **She ...**
4. It's getting rather cold in here. **I ...**
5. I don't know what's wrong with my car. **It ...**
6. I have no idea how your mobile phone works. **... you ...?**
7. I asked Alan to lend me his camera, but **he ...**
8. I've got this letter from that hotel in Paris. **... you ...?**
9. My mother can say what she likes. **I ...**
10. It gets so cold and misty here in the autumn. **I ...**
11. My father has this nasty cough all the time. **But he ...**
12. We're going to the US this summer. **We ...**

7 Life used to be quite different then ■ 73, 93, 94

Tommy's great-grandfather often tells him about the time when he was a boy.
Translate this into German, paying particular attention to the marked forms.

… In those days we **didn't use to have** hot water coming out of a tap whenever you wanted it. Every Saturday afternoon my mother **would boil** a big pot of water on the stove and pour it into a big tub in the kitchen. Then we children **would get** into the tub – one after the other – and we all **used** the same water of course. How **would** you **like** that, Tommy? Of course, once you've **got used to having** a warm shower every day, you forget how it **used to be** then. After the bath my mother **would put** fresh clothes out for us – and they **used to last** us the whole week. On Sundays we **would go** to church and, of course, we **would have to** keep our clothes clean until then. Yes, we **used to play** football, too. Often we **wouldn't have** a proper ball, so we **used** an old tin instead, or even a stone. And there **used to be** hardly any traffic, so we **would** often **play** football in the High Street. That **would be** difficult today, **wouldn't** it? Sometimes *my* great-grandfather **would tell** *me* what life was like when he was a boy. But if I told you that, you **wouldn't believe** it, Tommy.

8 Shall we? Are we supposed to? ■ 95

Complete what these people are saying, using **shall**, **should (have)**, **ought to (have)** *or* **be supposed to**. *(There is often more than one correct solution.) Choose from these expressions.*

bring food and drinks · *come at 9 o'clock* · *do exercises 3 to 8* · *fill the tank before* · *go and see* ✔ · *make an appointment* · *share or use public transport* · *switch the TV on*

1. Look, "The Last Paradise" is on at the Odeon. …
   Shall we go and see it?
2. There are simply too many single drivers going to work in their cars. …
3. Oh, no, we're running out of petrol in the middle of this tunnel. …
4. The news is coming on now. …
5. Old Batty gave us a lot of homework yesterday. …
6. What about Jenny's party on Saturday? …
7. The excursion was a bit of a fiasco. The coach was terribly late. It arrived at 10.30. …
8. I haven't been to the dentist's at all this year. …

9 You should have ... ■ 87, 88, 92, 95

ask worry leave home earlier ✔ watch go by bus wait apologize book seats be an accident take the wrong turning at that roundabout

Complete what these people say or think, using **needn't have**, **must have** *or* **should have**. *Choose from these expressions.*

1. I'll be late for my appointment. Damn! I ...
   I should have left home earlier.
2. You could have gone without me. You ...
3. That western on TV last night was great. You ...
4. Jim's bike is still in the garage. He ... after all.
5. Everything turned out OK after all. So we ...
6. I could easily have helped you with the move. You ...
7. Traffic doesn't usually get held up here. There ...
8. The whole thing was really my fault. I ...
9. Look, the theatre is only half full. We ...
10. This can't be the right road! We ...

"Hot? This? You should have been here last week."

10 Do you need some more time? ■ 96

Put these sentence parts together in a sensible way.

a	don't need ✔	**A**	ask her to pay for the tickets.
b	need	**B**	invite her to the party?
c	need to	**C**	to be washed. ✔
d	needn't	**D**	ask for any more.
e	needs to	**E**	be repaired.
f	dare	**F**	dive in from up there.
g	dared to	**G**	say so.
h	daren't	**H**	some help.
i	didn't dare to	**I**	you read it.

1. Surely these jeans are clean enough still. They ... *a + C*
2. I find this job rather difficult to do on my own. I ... ________
3. This car window doesn't close properly any more. It ... ________
4. Kate never has any money on her. You ... ________
5. You know I don't like Amy very much. Do we ... ________
6. Hey, this is a private letter. How ... ________
7. This morning I wanted to tell my boss he's a fool. But I ... ________
8. After losing all that money he hardly ... ________
9. The cliff is at least 10 meters high, and I don't know how deep the water is. I ... ________

"Do you wish to order now, or do you need some more time to add up the calories?"

Chapter 12 The verb and its objects

1 Words that can easily be confused ■ 97

Which verb is suitable? (Be careful with the forms.)

lie lay sit set rise raise

1. It was so noisy, he had to ______ his voice to make himself heard. 2. We won't need anyone to help us ______ the carpet *(Teppich)*, will we? 3. I'm not sure when to take the cake out of the oven. I forgot to ______ the timer. 4. She was ______ in bed, feeling ill. 5. I was so tired after lunch that I ______ down for half an hour. 6. Who do you ______ next to in class? 7. Where does the sun ______? – In the east, of course. 8. A young woman got on the bus and ______ down next to me. 9. I can ride my new bike better now that I've ______ the height of the saddle. 10. Let me tell you a story. There was once a goose that ______ golden eggs ... 11. The inflation rate ______ again last year. 12. He picked up the tea-pot and ______ it in the middle of the table.

2 What's that in German? ■ 97

Translate these sentences into German.

1. Kent is called the Garden of England because so much fruit is grown there.
2. Ben has grown a lot since I saw him last.
3. I'm afraid I don't know how to work this ticket machine.
4. I've put a new battery in my alarm clock, but it still doesn't work.
5. You shouldn't leave the tap running while you clean your teeth.
6. It's always been my father's dream to run a five-star hotel.

3 Using phrasal verbs ■ 98

a) Choose suitable phrasal verbs – in the right form – to complete the sentences.

look – after / round / out
get – over / off / on
put – off / away / up
take – away / out / over

1. We must ______ the bus at the next stop.
2. Your room is a real mess! Why don't you ______ all those clothes ______ in the cupboard?
3. Who's going to ______ your budgie while you're away?
4. I wouldn't ______ the dog's bone ______ if I were you!
5. I'm going to ______ those new shelves ______ in my room tomorrow. It's a job I've been ______ for ages.
6. You gave me such a shock, I haven't ______ it yet.
7. Can I help you, madam? – No, I'm not looking for anything special. I'm just ______.
8. ______! There's a car coming.
9. Have you ______ the dog ______ yet today? – No, it's been too wet!
10. Now that their father has died, Ben and Sal have ______ the family business.
11. I don't see my cousin much. To be honest, we don't really ______ very well.

b) Decide on the right word order. (If there are two possibilities, give them both.)

1. Won't you ______________________________? *(your coat – off – take)*
2. Can you go round to Sarah's house and ______________________________? *(her – up – pick)*
3. My hair is such a mess! ______________________________! *(it – at – look)*
4. I don't know this word. I'll have to ______________________________ *(it – up – look)*
5. Can I speak to Mr Slade? – One moment, I'll ______________________________ *(you – through – put)*
6. Ben, would you please ______________________________? *(the rubbish – out – take)*
7. The milk's gone sour. ______________________________! *(it – away – throw)*
8. I've decided to ______________________________ *(my appointment – off –*

4 Overheard at school ■ 99

Finish what these people are saying, putting the two objects in the most suitable position. Decide whether to use **to** *or not.*

things
a lift *a second piece* *it*
some textbooks *them✔* *them*
them *your biro*

people
me *Mike* *Mrs Fuller, the new secretary✔* *our guests*
three or four of you *the people in the back row*
those that haven't seen them yet *the people that have only had one*

1. I see you've all filled in those forms. Could someone take *them to Mrs Fuller, the new secretary*?
2. I haven't got anything to write with. Could you lend ______________________________?
3. I'm sorry, you can't have my bike tomorrow. I've already promised ______________________________.
4. Which of you are going to find it difficult to get to the theatre in time? I can offer ______________________________.
5. Today we've got some exchange students from America in our English lesson. Let's give ______________________________.
6. Don't keep all the texts here at the front. Please pass ______________________________.
7. Has everyone seen the photos? If not, could you show ______________________________?
8. Carol's birthday cake tastes super. Let's offer ______________________________.

5 Tuesday ■ 99

Write out the text, putting the objects in the place you think best and deciding whether to use **to** *or not.*

Tuesday was an ordinary workday for Sam Mogul, one of the managing directors at *Raptor Inc.*, the Californian high-tech giant. In the morning Sam said (*good-bye – his wife*). When he got to his office, he gave (*a kiss – Naomi, his favourite secretary*). Then he dictated (*a few business letters to their partners in South America – her*). That only took (*about half an hour – them*). Then he drove downtown to buy (*a $50.000 bracelet – his wife*), a little birthday present. When he got back, his second-in-command introduced (*a group of Japanese businessmen – him*). Naomi offered (*glasses of champagne – all of them*), and Sam started to describe (*the functions of the new Super-PC – his guests*), **explaining** (*all the advantages – them*). He mentioned the possibility of an evening out together, and they smiled politely when he suggested (*this – them*). In the afternoon, he met with some trade union officials and announced (*the firm's decision to lay off another 2000 workers – them*). He explained (*the reasons for these cuts – the angry officials*) and promised (*the firm's generous help – all of the workers*). At last he was able to show (*some of the city's sizzling nightlife – his Japanese friends*). The next morning his wife asked (*some questions about his workday – her husband*), but Sam didn't mention (*all the details – her*).

6 Your opinion, please! ■ 100

Express your opinion about these things. Use the verbs on the left (with or without **as**)*, and choose from the expressions on the right (or others of your own!) to give your opinion.*

regard (would) call look upon think consider (would) describe find accept | *as?* | *crazy a big threat to our planet fun great safe dangerous perfectly acceptable normal a problem a waste of time (un)important to my life ...?*

Example:

1. I regard global warming as a big threat to our planet.

1. global warning
2. computer games
3. most politicians
4. nuclear power
5. genetically modified products
6. women in the armed forces
7. extreme (high-risk) sports
8. smoking
9. science fiction films
10. job-sharing

"Sorry to call you out, doctor, but it never seems to happen during surgery hours."

7 Laughter really seems to be the best medicine ■ 101

Translate the article into English, using verbal expressions for the German adverbs.

Lachen, die beste Medizin

Der Forschungsbericht *(research report)* einer Gruppe amerikanischer Ärzte bestätigt *(to confirm)* eine alte Redensart *(saying)*: Lachen ist **anscheinend** wirklich die beste Medizin. Die Ärzte behaupten *(to claim)*, dass Menschen, die sich **gern** lustige Videos ansehen, **mit Sicherheit** viel weniger Herzanfälle bekommen *(to have a heart attack)* als andere. Sie haben außerdem herausgefunden, dass Menschen mit Herzproblemen allgemein weniger lachen. Solche Menschen erkennen **anscheinend** den Humor in vielen Situationen nicht, und dies wirkt sich **wahrscheinlich** negativ auf ihre Gesundheit aus *(to have a negative effect on)*.

„**Leider** wissen wir noch nicht genau, auf welche Weise das Lachen das Herz schützt," erklärte Dr. Eric Miller, der bekannte Herzspezialist. „Aber die Gründe werden **vermutlich** bald entdeckt. (**Zufälligerweise** arbeitet auch ein kanadisches Team gerade an derselben Frage)."

„Wir wissen, dass Menschen, die sich körperlich betätigen *(to exercise)*, nicht rauchen und fettarme (*lowfat*) Nahrung zu sich nehmen **mit Sicherheit** das Risiko eines Herzinfarkts reduzieren. **Hoffentlich** nehmen die Menschen auch das tägliche Lachen in diese Liste auf *(to add to)*."

Also dann: Wenn Sie hundert Jahre alt werden wollen *(to live to be a hundred)* freuen Sie sich [ruhig] **weiterhin** über diese blöden Videos *(to enjoy s.th.)*, die Sie **früher** heimlich angeschaut haben.

Chapter 13 The infinitive

1 What do they expect? ■ 102, 103, 105, 106

Decide who is speaking. Then make sensible sentences with the verbs on the right. Try to use each verb at least once.

our English teacher ✔	*Jack's sister*	*our coach*	*my driving instructor*
the police	*Jessica's parents*	*our neighbours*	*Tim's mother*

advise	*expect*	*ask*
warn	*tell*	*want*

1. "You should read as much English as possible." Our English teacher advises us to read as much English as possible.
2. "Please tell us who you're going out with." ____________
3. "Never leave bicycles unlocked." ____________
4. "Don't drive too fast near schools and playgrounds." ____________
5. "Please ask me before you borrow my things!" ____________
6. "Could you please keep your music low while our baby is sleeping?" ____________
7. "You needn't help me in the kitchen." ____________
8. "Don't eat too much before a match." ____________

2 What's *dass* in English? ■ 103–105

Translate these sentences, remembering that infinitive constructions are often used in English where dass *would be used in German.*

1. Wir gehen morgen in den Zoo, und wir möchten, dass ihr mitkommt.
2. Man kann nicht erwarten, dass die Löwen die ganze Zeit brüllen.
3. Ich warte immer noch darauf, dass der Eisbär *(polar bear)* ins Wasser springt.
4. Es ist wichtig, dass die Tiere regelmäßig gefüttert werden.
5. Meiner Meinung nach ist es falsch, dass Tiere in Gefangenschaft *(captivity)* gehalten werden.
6. Die Schimpansen *(chimpanzees)* sind nicht nahe genug, dass wir sie fotografieren können.
7. Der Affe hier will, dass ich ihm meine Banane gebe.

"And if you want me to roar, it's an extra £5."

3 Easy for you to do! ■ 104

Rewrite these sentences, using **for** *+ infinitive. The meaning should stay the same.*

1. We're still waiting, but the pub hasn't opened yet.
   We're still waiting for the pub to open.
2. I'm afraid I can't come to Scotland with you – it's just not possible. __________

"I think they're waiting for us to dance."

3. American tourists don't often come to this part of the world – it's quite unusual. __________
4. The weather is often windy here at this time of year – that's normal. __________
5. Will it be all right if we visit you in August? __________
6. Don't ring us up while you're away – there's no need. __________
7. Here's a key that you can use if we should be out. __________

4 Tips from a teenage magazine ■ 107

Which is right, **let** *or* **make**?

1. If you're feeling a bit low, watch a really funny video with a friend. That'll __________ you laugh, and as you know, laughing soon __________ you feel better.
2. You may not believe it, but maybe that boy of your dreams likes you, too! He might just be too shy to __________ you know.
3. Nobody can __________ you take drugs if you don't want to. Don't __________ other people persuade you!
4. Find a good hairdresser. A really good haircut will __________ your hair look great! Even if you want to __________ your hair grow long, you should still go every two months or so.
5. Don't __________ yourself be fooled by that good-looking girl. She's probably flirting with other boys, too. Remember, if she's __________ you feel so unhappy, she's definitely not the one for you!
6. Try not to get back home later than your parents allow. If you __________ this happen too often, your parents may __________ you come home earlier next time – or they may not even __________ you go out at all!

5 Perception and observation ■ 108

Complete what these people are saying, using verbs of perception and observation, and infinitives.

notice hear see feel watch

leave play come in take sting give touch ring

1. Joanna must have gone home. Funny! Nobody ______________________.
2. That was the doorbell. Didn't you ______________________?
3. He was shoplifting! I ______________________ that CD!
4. Our team are playing really well this season. Will you come with me and ______________________ in the match on Saturday?
5. You were so quiet. I didn't ______________________.
6. Please don't feed the dog at the table. I ______________________ her a piece of cheese a moment ago.
7. Ouch! That stupid wasp! I didn't ______________________ my leg at first, but I certainly ______________________ me!

6 The Perfect English School ■ 109

These are some of the questions people ask us at *The Perfect English School.* And we can answer all of them!

When do I use the simple past and when the present perfect?
How can I increase my word power? ✔
Where must I put the adverbs in a sentence? I never know.
How can I learn to speak fluent English?
How can I avoid making mistakes?
How should I prepare for my exams?
Do I say "look nice" or "look nicely"? I've no idea.
It's so silly. I always put commas in the wrong places.

Complete these sentences, using infinitives after question words.

1. If you wonder *how to increase your word power*, we can recommend our efficient word power exercises.
2. If you don't know ______________________, we'll teach you how to use different tenses.
3. If you wonder ______________________, we'll explain the English word order to you.
4. If you'd like to know ______________________, we'll show you ways to reduce them.
5. If you've no idea ______________________, we'll explain the difference between adjectives and adverbs.
6. If you're not sure ______________________, our conversation classes are just the thing for you.

7. If you can't remember ______________________________,

   we'll tell you the rules of punctuation in English.

8. If you wonder ______________________________,

   we'll give you useful tips for revision work.

7 The way to start a class war? ■ 110–112

Replace the marked clauses by infinitive constructions.

In the past, if Americans wanted to see identically dressed schoolchildren, **Britain was the country that they had to go to.**
This is no longer so. Today, the school round the block is the school **you should look at.**
Long Beach in California was the first district **that pioneered school uniforms**. And Philadelphia is the first big city **that has made uniforms obligatory in all its schools.** But it is no longer the only one **that asks parents to buy uniforms for their children.**
So for many American parents, school uniform will soon be the most expensive item **that they will have to buy for school**. Poor inner-city Americans are not the only people **that complain about this new trend.**
Kate Singleton, 16-year-old high school student, says: "In Britain school uniforms are traditionally worn **so that social differences are disguised.** But here in America everybody is free and equal, and school uniforms would be the best way **in which creativity and individuality would be killed**. I'll be the last person **that ever wears those Mickey Mouse costumes**."
But many students disagree. For them wearing school uniform is a good way **in which they can show a sense of identity and commitment to the school.**
So, as with so many disputes in America, the courts may be the place **where this question is decided.**

⁂ 8 To tell the truth ... ■ 101–113

Translate this television discussion into German.

Presenter: And here is "In Focus" again. To start with, let's say hello to our guests tonight: Sue Pendleton from the Labour Party and Michael Atkinson from the Conservatives. Of course, the result of this debate is wide open, and it remains to be seen ...

Sue: Well, to be honest, what Michael has said about our policies does not correspond to the facts. I'm the last person to suggest that such things ought to be brushed under the carpet. And, to be fair, there appear to have been some – hm – misunderstandings. It is to be expected that ...

Michael I'm sorry, Susan, but you seem to have misunderstood us completely. To tell you the truth, your party always tries to make the figures appear in a better light. But, generally speaking, the voters want the parties to tell them the truth. Well, to cut a long story short ...

Sue. To claim that we tell the voters lies is an insult. And I'm waiting for Michael to apologize for it. He is unlikely ever to understand what the real world is like. You just have to look around you to see how bad things have become. But I'm not the only one to have realized ...

Presenter: I'm afraid I'll have to interrupt the two of you here. To sum up, I thank you both for the lively and informative discussion. Our two candidates are certain to have made it easier for you to decide at the next elections. "In Focus" is *the* programme for politically interested people to watch. Good night.

"To tell you the truth, I'm getting sick of rain!"

Chapter 14 The gerund

1 Tiger Woods ■ 115, 116, 119, 120

When Tiger Woods was 18, he was already famous as an amateur golf champion. But when his parents tried to get tickets for the three of them for the US Masters golf competition in Augusta, Georgia in 1994, they were told there were no more left. The Woods family knew the reason: Earl Woods was black, his wife Asian, and their son of mixed race.

What the Golf Club committee thought in 1994:

- We don't want non-whites to come to the club!
- They may mix with the spectators!
- People may object!
- Some of our members are sure to complain!
- Blacks might even come into the club house!
- Trouble would probably start!
- Some members might even leave the club!
- We don't want our old traditions to change!

Now use the "object + gerund" construction to explain their feelings. Choose from these expressions.

not like be afraid of not be keen on be against hate the idea of

They didn't like non-whites coming to the club.

INFO: Three years later, in 1997, Tiger Woods played in the Masters himself – and at the age of 21 became the youngest player and the first non-white ever to win it.

2 Ever tried surfing? ■ 117

Surfing is very popular, not only in California and Australia, but also in Britain.
Complete what these young people at a surf school in North Devon say to a newspaper reporter, deciding whether to use gerunds or infinitives.

Lucy: We couldn't wait ________ *(get)* into the water! But actually, if you mean ________ *(learn)* how ________ *(surf)* properly, you need ________ *(start)* with the "dry land basics". That means ________ *(check)* the sea for jetties[1] or rocks. And you mustn't forget ________ *(check)* there's no red flag flying – that tells you it's dangerous ________ *(surf)* or ________ *(swim)*.

Tom: Before we started on our first day, we had to practise on the beach, with our boards on the sand. Quite a few people stopped ________ *(watch)* us, we must have looked so funny! We tried ________ *(do)* everything right, and soon our instructor said we could try ________ *(practise)* in the water. I'll never forget ________ *(try)* ________ *(stand)* up on the board the first time. Impossible! I thought I'd never learn! But I didn't stop ________ *(practise)*. Soon we all started ________ *(improve)*.

Sophie: When you get on the board, you must remember ________ *(keep)* your knees bent. Not easy! But the most difficult thing is trying ________ *(judge)* when the wave is going to break. I can remember ________ *(practise)* again and again before I succeeded! Our instructor is fabulous – and the course has been really great. I'll never regret ________ *(come)* here and ________ *(take)* part.

[1] **jetty** *Mole, Landesteg*

3 The problem of phobias ■ 115–118

Replace the marked phrases by phrases with gerunds. Use these verbs.

avoid	*can't stand*	*dream of*	*end up*	*go on*	*hate*	*imagine*
insist on	*look forward to*	*mean*	*rely on*	*stop*	*succeed in*	
start	*start*	*think of✓*	*worry about*			

Do you start to panic when you think of touching a spider? ...

Do you start to panic **at the thought that you might touch** a spider? Do you **begin to sweat** when you **think to yourself that you are going up** an escalator? In Britain alone there are millions of people with phobias, who **are troubled and unhappy when they think that they may have to do** things that other people do not find frightening at all.
Some people **find it extremely unpleasant to look at** raw meat. Others **dislike it extremely when they are** in a dark place. **The consequence of this can be that they are unable** to spend the night away from home in case they cannot find a light switch.
Michelle's case is typical; she **first felt frightened of** escalators when she was a small child. Twenty years later this fear turned into a phobia. At first she **tried not to go** by tube. Then she **no longer went** to any places where there might be a lot of stairs. "Even **in my dreams, when I went** on an escalator, I woke up shaking all over," she says. "In the end I needed treatment."
Lots of people like Michelle **need to take** drugs. But if **they continue to take** pills over a long period, they may **in the end become addicted**. Doctors **demand from their patients that they face** their fears. A specialist at one of Britain's treatment centres says: "When once you **have managed to let** that hairy spider run up your arm, you have beaten your particular phobia and you can **be optimistic and expect to lead** a normal life again."

"Write a story on how number 8 feels about having 3 subtracted from it."

4 The idea of sunbathing ... ■ 119, 120

Rewrite the sentences, using gerund constructions.

At Shanklin[1] one has to adopt the detestable custom of bathing in drawers[2]. If ladies don't like to see men naked why don't they keep away from the sight.
(The Rev Francis Kilvert, 1874)

1. Because of the supposed healing qualities of the cold water, people in the 18th and 19th centuries liked to go to the seaside. (*be interested in*)
   Because of the supposed healing qualities of the cold water, people in the 18th and 19th centuries were interested in going to the seaside.
2. But in those days people didn't want to lie in the sun. (*be keen on*)
3. A dark skin was associated with low class. This was because the only people that always worked outside were peasants. (*be used to*)
4. By the 1920s rich Americans were eager to go to the fashionable South of France. (*be crazy about*)
5. And back home they felt good when they showed off their suntan – now a status symbol for the rich. (*be proud of*)
6. Today we are no longer surprised to see millions of sunbathers on European beaches. (*get used to*)
7. On those beaches, people can drop some of their everyday boundaries, like shyness or social class. (*opportunity of*)
8. And today nobody feels embarrassed to drop all their clothes, too. (*not feel ashamed of*)
9. But in some places – like Brazil or the US – people don't go topless. This is out of the question. (*idea of*)
10. And in many hot countries, people don't find it easy to understand how anyone can lie in the heat for hours on end. (*difficulty in*)
11. Today, with the shrinking of the ozone layer, people realize that it is dangerous to be in the sun too long. (*danger of*)
12. So perhaps in the future, people will no longer want to lie in the sun to get a suntan because they fear they might get skin cancer. (*get tired of – be afraid of*)

(based on an article in *The Guardian*)

[1] **Shanklin** seaside resort in the Isle of Wight– [2] **drawers** underpants

5 Please don't feed the wildlife ■ 114, 119–121

Translate the text into German, paying particular attention to the gerund constructions.

We, as visitors, have just as important **a role in managing** our national parks as do national park managers. **Feeding wildlife** is a classic example of how good intentions can upset the ecological balance.
It has long been known that wildlife quickly **get used to being fed** by humans. But once they **have got used to eating** human food, animal stomachs will only contain the bacteria **necessary for digesting** human food. When the tourist season ends and winter sets in, these animals will have **difficulty in finding** food at all, or – if they do – might be **in danger of starving** to death with full stomachs.
Worse yet, **feeding** can cause normally docile animals like deer to become aggressive. In one sad instance, a young child was killed by a deer buck when he wanted to eat his sandwich himself **instead of giving** it to the animal.
Of course, children are **fond of feeding** those cute animals, but **giving in** just once to the big, brown pleading eyes can have tragic consequences. Be responsible! Learn to be a friend of wildlife **by not trying** to befriend animals with food.

(adapted from the Bryce Canyon National Park magazine HOODOO)

6 On patrol at a London school ■ 121

Improve the text by rewriting the marked sentences with the help of gerund constructions. Choose from these prepositions.

after   apart from   as well as   by   for   in spite of   instead of   without

A school in London has now become the first to copy America by having its own police officer.

A school in London has now become the first to copy America: it has its own police officer. Police Constable Andy Briers, 34, has now got his office at Northumberland Park School, in one of London's toughest areas. In one incident last term, four teenage girls not from the school came into the building with two enormous kitchen knives; **in another case a boy nearly died after he was attacked by fellow pupils[1]. PC Briers not only sends off gangs of intruders[2], he also makes truancy[3] patrols and sends pupils back to lessons. He has been with the police for seven years, and he is a qualified PE teacher, too.**
So far he has had a good influence on the school, and the staff[4] accept him. **He has been there for a few weeks now – and hasn't had to arrest a pupil at all.** "You can sort out most problems at school," he said. **"But I would arrest pupils if they brought weapons to school or took drugs."**
Although he is disliked by some pupils, he is already on first-name terms with many. Thanassi, 18, from a Greek family, said: "Security has improved a lot. And we really like Andy." **His presence builds people's confidence in the police; it is not seen as a threat.**

(adapted from *The Times*)

[1] **fellow pupil** *Mitschüler* – [2] **intruder** *Eindringling* – [3] **truancy** *Schulschwänzen* – [4] **staff** *hier: die Lehrer*

7 How about doing this exercise? ■ 122

Complete what these people are saying, using gerunds after **it's no use**, **it's no good**, **there's no**, **what / how about?** *or* **it's (not) worth**. *Choose from these verbs:*

book seats   deny it   eat out   go there   know   phone now   read✔   wait

1. Her new novel is really exciting. *It's worth reading.*
2. I don't feel like cooking today. ______________________________?
3. It's very late now. I don't think they'll come. ______________________________.
4. Sarah is never in at this time of day. ______________________________.
5. We all know you were in the room when the murder was committed. ______________________________.
6. I can't tell how she'll react when you ask her. ______________________________ what she'll say.
7. I don't know whether they'll still have tickets on Sunday. ______________________________.
8. London is a fascinating city. ______________________________.

Chapter 15 Participles

1 Stay switched on, please ■ 124

Complete the sentences with these verb pairs. Use the present or past participle form of the second verb.

come / run	*stay / chat*	*remain / close*
stay / connect	*stand / wait*	*sit / watch*
go / crash	*lie / stretch out*	

1. There were a lot of passengers for the Edinburgh train. They ______________________ on the platform for the train to come in.
2. He never goes out in the evenings. He just ______________________ TV the whole time.
3. Our dog doesn't like going out much in this cold weather. She prefers ______________________ in front of the fire!
4. Due to the cold weather, the open-air swimming pool had to ______________________ until the middle of June.
5. I really must go now. I can't ______________________ here any longer!
6. The car skidded off the road and ______________________ into a tree.
7. Kate can't seem to decide anything for herself. She always ______________________ to me for advice.
8. As members of the Commonwealth, it is possible for many independent countries to ______________________ to Britain.

2 Experiences ■ 125, 126

Complete the sentences with the verbs on the right. Decide whether to use participles or infinitives.

1. *John, on holiday in Cornwall:* I noticed a man with a camera ____________ out on a rock with his back to the sea. I watched him ____________ a photo of some sea-birds. Then, to my horror, I saw an enormous wave ____________ up behind him and ____________ him off the rock into the sea.

   come
   knock
   stand
   take

2. *Becky, a passenger on the London Underground:* I noticed a lot of people ____________ on the train at Westminster. Shortly before the next stop, I felt someone ____________ into me from behind. I couldn't tell who it was, but I could feel people ____________ from all sides all the time. A moment later, I saw the doors ____________. Then I noticed a small girl ____________ through the crowd with my handbag under her arm!

   bump
   get
   open
   slip
   push

3. *Fiona, a Glasgow schoolgirl:* I heard a car suddenly ____________ round the corner behind me. I had already noticed some children ____________ in the road. Now I heard the car's brakes ____________. Too late! I saw it ____________ straight into the group of kids. It was sickening. Next moment I could hear someone ____________.

   come
   drive
   play
   scream
   screech

4. *Sam, on the evening of his first day in Australia:* We felt the day ______________ cooler at last! Now we could see the shadows ______________ on the grass. We sat down on a big red rock and watched the sun ______________ in brilliant colours over the distant hills. We could even hear budgies ______________ in the trees! It was marvellous. Then, to make a perfect end to a perfect day, we saw a little group of kangaroos suddenly ______________.

appear
get
lengthen
set
sing

3 What's that in English? ■ 127

✎ *Remember that the German verb* **lassen** *has a number of equivalents in English.*

1. Deine Haare sehen super aus! – Danke! Ich habe sie gestern schneiden lassen.
2. Warum lässt du dein altes Fahrrad nicht reparieren?
3. Soll ich das Fenster zumachen? – Nein, lassen wir's noch eine Weile offen.
4. Unsere Lehrer lassen uns ganz schön hart arbeiten.
5. Sandra hat ihren Fotoapparat im Bus liegen lassen.
6. Was war los? Warum hast du uns so lange warten lassen?
7. Bitte lassen Sie uns wissen, ob Sie das Angebot annehmen wollen.
8. Möchten Sie Ihre Jacke ausziehen? – Nein danke, ich lasse sie an.
9. Diese Hose ist leider nicht waschbar. Ich muss sie immer reinigen lassen.
10. Wir haben heute den Hund zu Hause gelassen. Er wollte uns aber erst gar nicht gehen lassen.

"Never mind the delay – you've got your car cleaned."

4 The new Americans ■ 128

✎ *Replace the participle constructions in this text by relative clauses.*

In the 19th century, America was an enormous magnet, **drawing** people into it from every direction. There were two distinct waves of immigrants **entering** the US. The first phase, **lasting** until about 1880, is called the "old immigration". Most of those immigrants were farmers, often **leaving** behind poverty or famine. These people, **attracted** by the availability of land, settled mainly in the Midwest and the Great Plains.
In the 1880s, there came another wave of immigrants, **known** as the "new immigration". These immigrants were mostly Catholics and Jews **coming** from southern and eastern Europe.
The new immigrants – **encouraged** by new immigration laws, by the new steamship service **opened** between America and Europe and by letters **sent** from people who had gone before – moved to the US in search of greater economic opportunity. The excitement **felt** by immigrants **coming** to the New World was mixed with anxiety and fear. The immigrants **landing** in New York had to pass through the immigration centre on Ellis Island, **set** up by the federal government in 1892.These newcomers, **bringing** with them the various cultures of Europe, broadened the cultural life of American cities.
One of those immigrants was a composer, **born** in Russia and **named** Baline. Baline, better **known** as Irving Berlin, expressed his love for his new country in patriotic songs, **including** "God Bless America".

"Come, come, now! You surely wouldn't hit anyone wearing glasses!"

5 Robinson Crusoe ■ 128, 129

Shorten this text by using participle constructions instead of the marked phrases.

"Robinson Crusoe" is a novel by Daniel Defoe; **it was published in 1719. Although later the novel took on** an almost mythological status, it is based on a true story, **which was written** by A. S. Selkirk. Selkirk was a sailor **who was put ashore** on an uninhabited island in 1704 and **managed to survive** until his rescue in 1709.
It seems probable that Daniel Defoe got the idea for his book **after he had met** Selkirk in 1711.
In Defoe's story, Crusoe, a young man, goes to sea **though he has been warned** by his parents. He suffers a number of misfortunes **until he is finally shipwrecked** off South America. **After he has lived** on the island for 28 years, he is finally rescued. **While he is staying** on the island, Crusoe adapts to his alien environment **and demonstrates** the self-sufficiency **which was admired** so much by Defoe himself. **As it combines** typical characteristics of the adventure story and fascinating aspects of travel literature, the novel was an instant success. It has become one of the classics of English literature, **which is enjoyed** by both young and adult readers.

6 The "Boston Massacre" – 5 March 1770 ■ 130

a) Rewrite the text, making it sound less formal by replacing the participle constructions.
b) Translate the text into German.

British troops having been sent to defend British customs officials, the mood in Boston was tense and ugly. **The rumour having spread** that British soldiers had beaten up two Boston youths, an angry crowd gathered. Some Bostonians threw snowballs and sticks at a small contingent of British soldiers. **One soldier having been struck** by a stick and **thrown** to the ground, the others panicked and started to fire into the mass of civilians. In half a minute the street was empty – **the dead and wounded left** on the ground. Three Americans had been killed outright – among them Crispus Atticus, a runaway slave – **two others later dying** of their wounds. The authorities promised to punish those responsible for the "Boston Massacre". **A jury finding** the commander of the soldiers innocent, only two soldiers were arrested and branded on the thumb with the letter "M" – for manslaughter. But the British withdrew from Boston. **With the hated army gone,** the mood in Boston improved. Until the next incident: the Boston Tea Party.

Chapter 16 Subordinate clauses

1 George Washington ■ 132

Add the correct adverbial clauses to the given main clauses and conjunctions.

In 1775 George Washington became commander of the American Continental Army.

1. He had to adopt tough measures **because ...**
2. In July 1776 a new British army landed on Staten Island **while ...**
3. Most of the American defenders were in battle for the first time, **whereas ...**
4. Many of Washington's men longed to return to their farms and shops and drifted back home **whenever ...**
5. His soldiers were mostly poor, **since ...**
6. France wanted the British to lose, but the French hesitated to enter the war **until ...**
7. It would have been very difficult for the Americans to win the war **if ...**
8. The British began to withdraw **as soon as ...**
9. Washington retired to his estate at Mount Vernon **after ...**
10. In 1789 Washington became the first President of the United States, **although ...**

a) ...they realised that a defeat for Britain was possible.
b) ...wealthier people were able to buy their way out of military service.
c) ...the French had not joined them.
d) ...peace had been signed with Britain in 1783.
e) ...he refused to accept a salary.
f) ...the British were professional soldiers.
g) ...the independent-minded Americans were brave but undisciplined. ✔
h) ...they felt like it.
i) ...the Declaration of Independence was being debated in Congress.
j) ...the French fleet arrived off New York.

1. *g* 2. ___ 3. ___ 4. ___ 5. ___ 6. ___ 7. ___ 8. ___ 9. ___ 10. ___

2 Into space ... ■ 133, 134, 137, 138

Rewrite these sentences, using relative clauses. Sometimes there will be more than one way of doing this. Use commas only where necessary.

1. The first artificial satellite went into orbit round the Earth in 1957; it was called "Sputnik 1".
2. The Russian Yuri Gagarin was the first person to go up into space; he made one orbit of the Earth in 1961.
3. The moon is a hostile place; it has no atmosphere to keep the temperatures constant.
4. Great plains stretch over the moon; its surface is dotted *(übersät)* with huge mountains and craters.
5. The moon has no light of its own; we can only see it because it acts like a huge mirror reflecting light from the sun.
6. Over the years scientists have often tried to explain the formation of the moon; they have produced many theories for this.
7. Some have suggested that the moon may have originally been part of the Earth; a piece of it may have broken off millions of years ago.
8. Neil Armstrong was one of the crew of the Apollo 11 spacecraft; Americans are proud to remember him as the first person to set foot on the moon.
9. Huge distances separate our solar system from others; they are simply impossible for us to imagine.
10. If you could travel by plane to Proxima Centauri, the nearest star to our own solar system, it would mean a long journey – it would take two million years!
11. Our galaxy alone contains about 100 billion stars; all of these may have their own huge solar systems.
12. Our galaxy is an independent system of stars existing together in space; it is called the Milky Way.

3 Explaining what words mean ■ 135, 136

Use contact clauses to explain what these words mean. Sometimes you will need to use a preposition.

Examples: breakfast: *Breakfast is the meal you eat in the morning.*
a library: *A library is a place you can borrow books from.*

1. an exercise book
2. a garage
3. a microwave
4. a stranger
5. a backpack
6. a ticket machine
7. primary school
8. rent
9. a youth hostel
10. your mother tongue
11. a toothbrush
12. your homework
13. chopsticks
14. your favourite book
15. a mobile phone
16. a vacuum cleaner

4 Less formal, please! ■ 136

✎ *In an everyday context, it is important to avoid formal style. Change these over-formal sentences so that the relative clauses sound more natural.*

1. Please let me see those photos at which you are looking.
2. Look, that's the house in which we once lived.
3. Sarah is the girl with whom you saw me playing tennis yesterday.
4. I don't think I've ever met the people about whom you were talking just now.
5. Where's the farm shop from which you always get your vegetables?
6. The 17th century is the period of history in which I'm especially interested.
7. The Jacksons? Are they the ones to whom you sent a card when we were in Greece?
8. Luckily, the weather is still something over which we have no control.

5 Working on Christmas Day ■ 133–139

*Complete the text with suitable relative pronouns (**who, which** or **whose**). Add **that** as an alternative wherever possible. Put brackets ( ) round any of the relative pronouns that can be left out.*

Sandra Brook, ______________ is 28, is a nurse ______________ works in the Accident and Emergency Department of a west London hospital. Unlike most of the people ______________ she knows, Sandra will be working on Christmas Day – from 8 a.m. to 8.30 p.m. It will not be the first Christmas Day ______________ she has spent working. Given the choice of working either over Christmas or the New Year, Sandra, ______________ parents live in Canada and ______________ closest friends will be spending the day with their families, has decided on the former, ______________ will mean that she will be free to celebrate the New Year with friends.

Sandra expects to be fairly busy on Christmas Day. "Illness and accidents aren't things ______________ just stop at Christmas!" she says. "GPs'[1] surgeries will be closed, of course, so people won't be able to go to the doctor ______________ they're used to. That means we'll see a few people ______________ have burnt their fingers on pots and pans while cooking the Christmas lunch. People of other religions ______________ don't celebrate Christmas may also come in because it's just a day like any other to them." The thing ______________ Sandra finds hardest to bear is when people die at Christmas. "I feel so sorry for the families because of the time of the year. But the saddest thing ______________ I've experienced is the number of people in hospital ______________ relatives don't visit them – or ______________ have no family at all." The nurses try to take extra time to talk to patients ______________ are obviously alone, and to help them join in the festivities. Gifts are donated to the hospital, ______________ ensures that nobody feels forgotten.

Does Sandra feel annoyed about having to work over Christmas? "Not at all. The good thing about this job is that you know you're helping people ______________ are in pain or distress. – And there's the evening ______________ I can look forward to. I'll be spending it with my boyfriend, John."

[1] **GP (general practitioner)** *Arzt für Allgemeinmedizin*

(adapted from *The Times Magazine*)

6 On holiday in Scotland ■ 139

a) Comment on these statements using clauses with **which** *and the sentences in the box.*

That's an advantage, of course.
So we don't get much sleep.
So we have to drive a long way to the nearest supermarket.✓
That makes him pretty boring.
That makes it very difficult to get there at night.
I find that far too much effort.
That makes it hard to understand people.
So I certainly won't go swimming.

1 There aren't any shops near our cottage, *which means that we have to drive a long way to the nearest supermarket.*

2 The Scottish accent around here is very strong, ______

3 It's only a short walk to the beach, ______

4 But the water is terribly cold, ______

5 Our neighbours have hundreds of chickens, and their cocks wake us up at 4 a.m., ______

6 Their son Colin looks very nice, but he is only interested in football, ______

7 The nearest disco is 10 miles away, ______

8 My parents always want me to go on long hikes with them, ______

b) Make your own comments.

1. My birthday will be on a Sunday this year, which ______
2. Fiona has got into the final, which ______
3. Joe has lost his mobile phone, which ______
4. Emma forgot to set her alarm clock last night, which ______

7 Whatever you say ■ 140

Fill in **whoever**, **whatever** *or* **whichever**.

1. I won't believe her in future, ______ she may say.
2. I've ordered some haggis, ______ that may be.
3. ______ said that has absolutely no idea.
4. Chelsea, Aston Villa? ______ of the two wins on Saturday, neither will have much chance in the Cup Final.
5. There isn't much choice. Just ice cream or chocolate pudding. So have ______ you prefer.
6. It's not a secret. You can tell ______ you like.

Chapter 17 Statements, questions, shortened sentences

1 Surely not! ■ 141

Correct these statements by making them negative. (Add the correct facts if possible.)

1. New York is the capital of the USA.
   New York isn't the capital of the USA. (Washington DC is the capital.)
2. Wales is part of England.
3. Shakespeare was born in London.
4. Daniel Defoe wrote "Treasure Island".
5. James Bond works for the FBI.
6. At the end of the Industrial Revolution everyone in England had a car.
7. The Winter Olympic Games have often been held in Scotland.
8. The Irish drive on the right.
9. Today a lot of prisoners are kept in the Tower of London.
10. Every single one of the famous Boat Races on the Thames has been won by Manchester University.
11. "Nessie", the Loch Ness monster, has been caught and can now be seen in London Zoo.
12. Black Americans are called "Native Americans".
13. Henry VIII had eight wives. (That's why he is called Henry VIII.)
14. The Indians had horses long before Columbus discovered America.

2 Do not enter ■ 142

Use positive or negative imperatives or **Let's** *in these situations. (Sometimes there are several possibilities.)*

Example:

1.

2.

3.

4.

5.

6.

3 Getting to know the neighbours ■ 143

There are some new people in one of the houses near where Mr Nosy lives. He's heard quite a bit about them and is talking to a friend, trying to find out more. Ask his questions.

1. know well? *Do you know them well?*
2. man and woman married? __________
3. daughter not called Jeannette? __________
4. go to comprehensive school? __________
5. father not work in Brussels? __________
6. not live in France before? __________
7. mother not French? __________
8. speak any English? __________
9. no car? __________
10. have a dog? __________
11. members of the tennis club? __________
12. paint house themselves? (looks awful) __________
13. I – too nosy? __________

4 Henry VIII ■ 144

Ask questions with question words about the marked phrases.

1. Henry VIII became King of England **in 1509.**
   When did Henry VIII become King of England?
2. He had been married to Katharine of Aragon **since 1501.**
3. Before she married Henry she had been **his brother Arthur's** wife.
4. Many years later Henry wanted a divorce from Katharine **because Katharine had failed to produce a male heir and because he had fallen in love with Anne Boleyn.**
5. But **the Pope** refused to grant Henry the divorce.
6. At that time the Catholic Church was very rich. It owned **more than a third** of the land in England.
7. **By persuading Parliament to make him Supreme Head of the Church in England,** Henry managed to get his divorce.
8. The power **of the Pope** had come to an end in England now.
9. All in all Henry had **six** wives.
10. **Two** of his wives were executed (Anne Boleyn and Catherine Howard); **two** of them were divorced (Katharine of Aragon and Anne of Cleves); **one** died while still married to Henry (Jane Seymore) and **the last one** (Catherine Parr) survived him.

5 *Which, what* or *who*? ■ 144

Decide which of the three to use.

1. ___________ shall we have for supper tonight? Shall we make a curry?
2. Ham salad or cheese? ___________ would you like?
3. Let's eat out this evening. ___________ time does Mario's open?
4. ___________'s going to help make the fruit salad?
5. ___________ would you like to drink? – Well, ___________ drinks have you got?
6. They've got lots of different cheeses, look. ___________ of them shall we get?
7. There's just one piece of cake left.
   ___________ of you wants to have it?
8. ___________ forgot to put the butter back in the fridge? Look how soft it's gone!
9. I even got some paper serviettes for the party. – ___________ colour did you get?
10. ___________ of us is going to do the washing-up? – You can. I did it yesterday.

"What we now have to decide is – which of us has run out of food?"

6 Your dog doesn't bite, does he? ■ 145, 146

Add question tags and short answers.

1. You've got a dog, ______________________? – Yes, ______________________.
2. Her name is Sandy, ______________________? – No, ______________________. *His* name is Rover.
3. You don't often go for walks with him, ______________________? – Yes, ______________________. Every day.
4. And he sometimes bites people, ______________________? – No, ______________________. He's never bitten anyone so far.
5. You wanted to take him on the excursion last week, ______________________? – Yes, ______________________. But my parents were against it.
6. Rover isn't allowed to sleep on your bed, ______________________? – No, of course ______________________.
7. Let's take him to the park this afternoon, ______________________? – OK, ______________________.
8. Come to my house at 4 o'clock, ______________________? – Yes, ______________________.
9. He can't do any funny tricks, ______________________? – Yes, ______________________. You'll be surprised.
10. You'll show me this afternoon, ______________________? – Sure, ______________________. And then you'll see how clever he is.

7 Do you agree? ■ 147

You are talking to a friend at school. React to her / his statements, saying that it's the same with you (=) or that you differ (≠).

1. I'm terribly hungry. – (=) ______________________.
2. I haven't had any breakfast this morning. – (=) ______________________.
3. I didn't understand the maths homework. – (≠) But ______________________. I thought it was quite easy.
4. I watched "Space Cowboys" on TV last night. – (=) ______________________.
5. I thought it was a fantastic film. – (≠) ______________________, though. I thought it was stupid.
6. I've been invited to Tina's birthday party. – (=) ______________________.
7. I haven't bought her a present yet. – (=) ______________________.
8. I never know what to get for people. – (=) ______________________.
9. I'd like to play tennis this afternoon. – (=) ______________________. Well, let's play together.

Chapter 18 From sentence to text (linking and emphasis)

1 Falling to the Earth from 12,000 feet ■ 148

Fill in suitable conjunctions and adverbs to link the sentence parts.

and ✓ but for however

1. It was the last day of my skydiving training course in California, ___and___ it was my 27th jump, ____________ I was still scared! It had been an intense week, ____________ I had been constantly confronted with my terrible fear of heights; ____________, I wouldn't have missed it for the world.

anyway either or for nevertheless neither nor yet

2. Stepping out of a plane two miles up in the air is ____________ pleasant ____________ easy. ____________, I somehow managed to live with my fear. I found the best way was to step out quickly; ____________ I realized that I ____________ had to act fast ____________ I wouldn't be able to act at all! I soon got used to it ____________, ____________ my fear was always there with me.

after all and and or therefore too

3. Actually, there is no *real* need to feel worried ____________ scared; ____________, you have two instructors firmly holding onto you at the beginning, ____________ you are in safe hands. They make sure you pull your ripcord[1] at the right height, ____________ they help you to get into the right "flying" position, ____________. Then, after 45 seconds of "free fall", your parachute opens ____________ (with a bit of luck) you land gently on the ground!

and and also on the one hand on the other hand so though

4. Learning to skydive in California rather than back home in Britain has advantages and disadvantages. ____________, the weather is so much better, ____________ you can be sure to finish the course in a week; ____________, it costs a lot more. The price includes the flight to Los Angeles, ____________, ____________ it ____________ includes the hotel, transport from the airport, ____________ so on.

(adapted from *The Guardian*)

[1] **ripcord** the "string" that lets the parachute out of its pack

2 Can you do this, too? ■ 148.2

Put in suitable equivalents of German **auch**.

1. The first inhabitants of North America were called "Indians" by the European settlers; now they are __________ called "Native Americans". 2. Indians fought with bows and arrows and with knives; many __________ carried tomahawks. Later they used rifles __________. 3. The Indians used buffalo skins for clothing, and for making tepees, __________. 4. Indians from one tribe often didn't know about other tribes' traditions. They didn't understand each other's languages __________. 5. The Pueblos, and the Cherokee Indians, __________, were peaceful tribes, unlike the Sioux, who were known for their fighting skills.

3 At the beach ■ 149

Use the **there** *construction to describe the scene. Use participles wherever suitable.*

There are lots of people (lying) on the beach. There ...

4 What's wrong here? ■ 150

Give the correct facts, using the **it is / it was** *construction.*

1. George Stephenson developed the steam engine in the 18th century, didn't he? *(James Watt)*
   No, it was James Watt who developed the steam engine in the 18th century.
2. Abraham Lincoln was the first American president, wasn't he? *(George Washington)*
3. Columbus sailed to America in 1592, didn't he? *(1492)*

4. In 1770 James Cook claimed the east coast of America for Britain. *(the east coast of Australia)*
5. Napoleon was finally defeated at the Battle of Trafalgar in 1815. *(the Battle of Waterloo)*
6. World War I started in 1939, didn't it? *(World War II)*
7. Captain Scott won the "race" to the South Pole, didn't he? *(the Norwegian Amundsen)*
8. Scott and his men all died on their way to the South Pole. *(on their way back)*
9. The US state of Virginia was called after Queen Elizabeth II, wasn't it? *(Queen Elizabeth I, "the Virgin Queen")*
10. The Americans were the first to send a man into space, weren't they? *(the Russians)*

5 Do ■ 151

React to these situations, using emphatic **do**.

1. Your teacher thinks you didn't learn your words. *Correct her.*

   ____

2. Your best friend has a new hairstyle. *Make a compliment.*

   ____

3. Two friends of your parents' have arrived. *Offer them a seat.*

   ____

4. The concert yesterday was great. *Explain your feelings.*

   ____

"Do let's buy it, Geoffrey."

5. Your mother thinks you don't want to help her. *Correct her.* ______________________________
6. Your brother and his friend are making an awful noise. *Tell them not to.* ______________________________

6 Journey across Australia ■ 152

In 1860, Robert Burke and William Wills were the first to try to cross the continent of Australia, from south to north, wanting to win the prize of £2,000 offered by the government of South Australia. But right from the start there were problems ...

✎ *Change the sentences, using inversion, to add to the "drama" of the story.*

1. The expedition left Melbourne in August 1860; but almost immediately, trouble started. *(hardly ... when ...)*
2. Burke, the leader, knew almost nothing about big expeditions; he was also a very impatient man. *(not only ... but ...)*
3. At first there were 16 men. But when they had gone about a quarter of the way, nine of them returned to Melbourne. *(scarcely ... when ...)*
4. Quarrelling had started among the men, and some of them were too slow for Burke. *(not only ... but ...)*
5. In November the Australian summer began. Then Burke and the others began to feel that they had chosen the wrong time of year for the expedition. *(not until ...)*
6. Because of the terrible heat, Burke and Wills took only two others the rest of the way north. But when they saw the Gulf of Carpentaria in front of them, they realized they could not reach the sea because the land in between was all swamp! *(no sooner ... than ...)*
7. The men hadn't ever felt so disappointed in all their lives. *(never ...)*
8. On the way back, heavy rain came down every day. The terrible weather slowed them down, and they all became dangerously ill. *(not only ... but ...)*
9. Then their food began to run out, and within a few weeks Burke and Wills and one of the other men had died. John King, the only one left, was lucky. Soon after the others died, he was discovered by a group of Aborigines who lived in the outback themselves. *(hardly ... when ...)*
10. Three months later, a search party from Melbourne came and found him. John King would not forget that day. *(never...)*

Chapter 19 Reported speech

1 It was out of this world! ■ 153, 155, 157

In May 2001 the world's first space tourist, 60-year-old Dennis Tito from California, returned from his week away from Earth.
First read what various people, including Tito himself, said about his trip.

- "This has been a life-changing experience for Dennis! I can't say if the Dennis Tito who returns to Earth will want the life he had before, or the love he had before. He may be quite a different person now!"
- "Mr Tito's trip has been a misuse of the spacecraft. The space station is for research, not for tourism."
- "I was worried at first that I might not feel good in space. But I felt great! In fact I've never felt better in my entire life."
- "We are satisfied with this flight. Mr Tito's trip may be just the start of extraterrestrial tourism."
- "The trip was out of this world! I just came back from paradise."
- "Mr Tito was great. He is not young, but he is a very strong and very proud man."
- "In future people won't have to pay as much as I did. When I get home, I'm seriously thinking of starting a company that will specialize in space flights for tourists."
- "I haven't adjusted to gravity yet! I'm still used to weightlessness."

Now report what was said, deciding who must have said what. The first reporting verbs are already given. To continue, you can use these:

go on to say add believe explain

1. When asked to describe his experience, Mr Tito was full of enthusiasm. He said ______________________________

____

2. When questioned about how he had felt in space, he admitted that ______________________________

____

____

3. When he dropped the apples traditionally given to cosmonauts on their return to Earth, he pointed out that

____

4. His girlfriend, worried about the effects space travel might have had on him, told reporters that __________

____

____

5. Mr Tito's Russian commander, when asked how he had managed on the International Space Station, was pleased to say that ____

____

6. Senator John Glenn, the veteran American astronaut, was critical, however. He was of the opinion that

____

7. But the Russian space officials, who see a commercial future in space tourism, informed the press that

____

____

8. Mr Tito's week in space cost him $ 20 million, but he emphasized that ______________________________

____

____

⁂ 2 Sarah's nightmare in jail ■ 153–155, 157

In her first interview since being released[1], 15-year-old Sarah (this is not her real name) told a newspaper reporter about the days she spent in prison. Here are some of the things she said.

"I'm just so glad to be home! I never want to go back to that place again, and I'll do everything I can to make sure I don't.

"This whole nightmare has taught me a huge lesson. Being in prison was the worst experience of my life, and I hope I won't ever go back. I'm never going to do anything else to risk that.

"What I did in November was stupid. My friends and I were feeling bored, and we lit a fire in a waste-bin to keep warm. But it got out of control and did a lot of damage. The police came, of course, and in the end there was a court case. I suppose the judge was just doing his duty when he sentenced[2] me. But it was a shock, nevertheless. I didn't even pack a bag when I went to court. I just hadn't realized he might send me to prison. He gave me 6 months. I couldn't believe it!

"I've been in Styal, one of Britain's toughest jails for women. I was the youngest of 15 teenagers there. I didn't like the prison food at all, and the clothes were awful. I was afraid of some of the women there, too. But I would like to thank the prison officers. They were really good, and they told my mum when she visited me that they'd look after me. In the end it was only six days! I've been released on bail[3]. The appeal[4] may be heard in a couple of months. Anyway, when I came out of the prison gate, my mum was standing there. It was great to see her. She took me to a McDonald's for a meal on our way home! Now I'm enjoying being at home. I just want to relax with my family and friends."

(adapted from *The Daily Telegraph*)

[1] **to release s.o.** *jdn. freilassen* – [2] **to sentence s.o.** *jdn. verurteilen* – [3] **on bail** *gegen Kaution* – [4] **appeal** *Revisionsverfahren*

✎ *First read carefully what Sarah said, then mark the points that seem most important. Finally, write a summary for a short newspaper report. In your report, try to vary the introductory verbs as much as you can. These verbs will be helpful to choose from:*

say explain think admit hope believe swear go on to say feel remember

3 What did he ask? ■ 156.1

At a lot of British schools, there is a careers officer who helps people to decide what kind of profession is likely to suit them best. When Anna talked to the careers officer at her school, he asked her a lot of questions. Here are some of them.

- ➤ Have you ever had a job of any kind?
- ➤ What did you like about your Saturday job, and what didn't you like?
- ➤ Do you enjoy working with other people, or can you work best on your own?
- ➤ Are you keen on solving problems?
- ➤ How good is your memory?
- ➤ What are your favourite subjects?
- ➤ Why do you like Maths so much?
- ➤ Would you be interested in going to University?
- ➤ Can you imagine working in an office or a bank?

Later, Anna's friend Judy wanted to know how her talk with the careers officer had gone.
✎ *What did Anna tell her?*

Anna: He asked me masses of questions! Most of them were quite general, really. First he asked me whether I . . .
Then he asked . . . He also wanted to know . . .

4 The Exe Estuary[1] Code ■ 156.2

The Exe Estuary is very popular in the summer months – with all sorts of people.
Look at these pieces of advice, and decide who they are addressed to. Then explain who is asked / advised / warned / told (not) to do what.

walkers birdwatchers fishermen dog owners✔ windsurfers and other water users swimmers

Be considerate to other estuary users. Always keep pets under control. Don't enter dog-free zones.

Dog owners are asked ____________________

____

____

Don't put yourself or others at risk. Be aware of the dangers from rising tides, and from cliff edges.

____

____

____

Never swim in the Navigation Channel. Don't enter the water in areas marked by red flags. Follow instructions on signs.

____

____

____

Fish wisely and avoid waste. Don't discard tackle[1], and return unwanted fish to the sea.

____

____

____

Do not disturb wildlife. Enjoy watching the wildlife, but keep your distance.

____

____

____

Keep to the appropriate area for your activity. Don't enter bathing areas. Keep noise to a minimum.

____

____

[1] **estuary** *Mündung* – [2] **tackle** *Angelzeug*

5 On the telephone ■ 155, 156

While Polly was in town with one of her friends after school one Friday afternoon, there were three phone calls for her back home. Her mother took the messages and told Polly about them when she came in.
First read what she told Polly.

1. "There was a call from David while you were out. He asked me to give you a message. He said there's going to be a barbecue at Mark's tonight, and he asked me whether you had mentioned it to me. Anyway, he said if you wanted, he would collect you at half past seven. He said he'd ring back later, though, unless you rang him."
2. "Nicola rang, too. She said she'd got your Physics book. She told me she'd taken it by mistake during afternoon school and hadn't discovered it until she got home. She said she'd give it back to you on Monday, and asked me whether I thought it would be all right."
3. "Then there was a call from Robin. He said he'd been trying to get tickets for the show tomorrow, but the line had been busy all the time, so he hadn't been able to book anything yet. He said there was no need for you to ring back."

✎ *Now write down what Polly's friends actually said on the phone. Be careful with the tenses, and with the pronouns.*

*"Welcome to the colony. That's odd – we always thought that **you** were **Mr** Brewster and that **you** were **Mrs** Brewster!"*

6 That's odd! ■ 155, 157

Things sometimes turn out differently from what you thought or expected. And people sometimes make mistakes or change their minds.
Use reported speech to react to what these people say, using your own ideas.

Examples: Debra isn't going to University after school. – But I thought *she wanted to study medicine.*

I can't finish these chips! – But you said *you were so hungry!*

1. I've decided to get my father a CD for his birthday. – But I thought ______________________

____

2. I'm afraid my train won't arrive till nearly midnight. – But you told me ______________________

____

3. The Priestleys have bought a flat in Kensington. – Are you sure? I thought ______________________

____

4. Ted will be going to Brazil for a year, so he'll have to brush up his Spanish. – Spanish? But I thought ______

5. I've asked Jenny to go to the cinema with me on Friday. – But only a few days ago you said ______

6. David wants to go into business with his elder brother. – That's odd. He told me ______

7. It's no good planning a picnic for tomorrow. It's going to be wet. – Surely not! When I watched the weather forecast, they said ______

8. Lucy's having a really big party. She's invited at least fifty people. – You must have got it wrong. She told me ______

7 Here and now – there and then ■ 158

Report what these people said (or say), being careful with the expressions of time and place.

1. *Ken (on Monday):* I'll ring you up tomorrow, Sue.

   Sue (a week later): Ken said ______

2. *Mayor:* The bypass will be built next year.

   Journalist (3 years later): The Mayor promised that ______

3. *Nicola (in London):* Living here is very expensive.

   Her mother (in Yorkshire): Nicola says that ______

4. *John:* I only got back to work two days ago, Sonia.

   Sonia (4 days later): John told me ______

5. *Doctor's receptionist:* I'm afraid Dr Philips will be away all next week.

   Patient (a week later): Dr Philips' receptionist told me ______

6. *Sam (on holiday in Cyprus, writing a postcard):* Sunday: Dear Liz and Joe, We arrived here yesterday …

   Joe (in Britain, a few days later): Here's a card from Sam! He says ______